Incredible

IF *YOU* GUESS THE STAR-SIGN OF THE AUTHOR . . .

Clues: Before writing for 'Spitting Image' and 'The Max Headroom Show', Tim John studied Psychology at Oxford University.

If that wasn't enough to warp his mind, he also wrote the recent Royal Comedy book, *Not Tonight Darling, I've Got A Hairdo*!!

If that wasn't enough to warp his mind, he also married a girl with the same star-sign as Thatcher, produced one daughter with the same star-sign as Hitler and another with the same sign as Brigitte Bardot. His mother was born under the same sign as Mussolini, his father under the same sign as Napoleon.

TO WIN AN *INCREDIBLE* PRIZE, just fill in the coupon below and send it to:

Editorial Dept,
Sphere Books Ltd,
27 Wrights Lane,
London W8 5TZ,
by January 1st, 1988.
The first correct entry drawn out of a hat will win our **fantastic** <u>mystery</u> prize.

Incredible Prize

Name...
Address...
Daytime telephone number ....
My star-sign is ....
I think Tim John is a ....
(anyone putting 'Wally' or 'Dickhead' doesn't get a prize.)

Also by Tim John in Sphere Books:

NOT TONIGHT DARLING, I'VE GOT A HAIRDO

TIM JOHN

SPHERE BOOKS LIMITED

This is a humorous book written by the author for the light-hearted entertainment of his readers and is not intended to cause offence to anyone.

First published in Great Britain by
Sphere Books Ltd, 27 Wrights Lane, London w8 5tz 1987
Copyright © 1987 by Tim and Jo John
Illustrations copyright © 1987 by David Hughes
TRADE
MARK

Set in 9½/11pt Trump and Helvetica by
Rowland Phototypesetting Ltd,
Bury St Edmunds, Suffolk

Printed and bound in Great Britain by
Cox and Wyman Ltd,
Reading, Berks

Introduction

Can there really be any future in fortune-telling?

Just look at how wrong even the most famous astrologers can be . . . 'a kind and generous man', with 'an excellent sense of humour', he 'offers warmth and hospitality wherever he goes'. That is how world-famous astrologer Teri King describes Taurus man. But Taurean men include Adolf Hitler! Of course, astrologers defend what is frequently just a load of old Taurus by saying that they *have* to be general because they don't have individual birth-charts for everybody. This is why we get such generalities as 'some of the world's greatest lovers have star-signs', 'nearly all Sagittarian bachelors are unmarried', or 'many Gemini women are female'!

Nevertheless, people always read into their horoscopes exactly what they want to hear. And people always read their horoscopes because everybody's favourite subject is themselves. With *Shock Horrorscopes* all that could change.

With hundreds of examples of your star-sign at its most shocking, you might well wish you were born under another. But there's no escape. Take the Taurus man/Libra woman relationship. How can you be sure they'll see eye to eye? Simple. Just look at two famous examples . . . Adolf Hitler (Taurus)/Maggie Thatcher (Libra). Can you think of a more compatible pair? So read on and discover the truth about yourself and those around you. And if you don't already know a person's star-sign, just turn to page 180, where you'll discover the thing that everybody desires . . . a sure-fire formula for telling absolutely anybody's true star-sign without having to look up their birthday . . .

SHOCK HORRORSCOPES

ARIES
The Sign of the Rampant. MARCH 21st – APRIL 20th.

TAURUS
The Sign of the Bullshitter. APRIL 21st – MAY 21st.

GEMINI
The Sign of the Two-faced Bastard. MAY 22nd – JUNE 21st.

CANCER
The Sign of the Crabby. JUNE 22nd – JULY 22nd.

LEO
The Sign of Pride and Prejudice. JULY 23rd – AUGUST 23rd.

VIRGO
Those Virgin on the Obscene. AUGUST 24th – SEPTEMBER 23rd.

LIBRA
The Sign of the Unbalanced. SEPTEMBER 24th – OCTOBER 23rd.

SCORPIO
The Sting in the Tail (i.e. pain in the arse). OCTOBER 24th – NOVEMBER 22nd.

SAGITTARIUS
The Sign of the Half-human. NOVEMBER 23rd – DECEMBER 21st.

CAPRICORN
The People who Get on your Goat. DECEMBER 22nd – JANUARY 20th.

AQUARIUS
The Sign of the Wetter Borer. JANUARY 1st – FEBRUARY 19th.

PISCES
The Sign of the Wet Dreamers. FEBRUARY 20th – MARCH 20th.

AQUARIUT
The Previously Undiscovered 13th sign of the Zodiac.

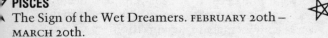

Star Sayings

ARIES: On being told that a rather prim English actress had no wish to work alongside a playboy like Aries Warren Beatty, he sent her flowers. To no avail. So he sent another, kinder letter. To no avail. So he wrote more kindly still. To no avail. So he sent a telegram saying, 'I suppose a fuck's out of the question?' No sign is on heat more than the first fire sign, Aries.

TAURUS: Taurean Victoria Wood once said that girls in her day 'weren't having hysterectomies every two minutes. If something went wrong down below, you kept your gob shut and turned up the wireless.' Never trust a Taurean doctor.

GEMINI: When Gemini Marilyn Monroe was once asked 'Do you really pose for photographers with nothing on?' she replied, 'Oh, no. I always leave the radio on.' Geminis are great truth-twisters.

CANCER: Cancerians never say anything worth quoting, though David Owen always hopes he will. Sylvester Stallone came close to saying 'Ugh!' once, but had elocution problems half-way through.

LEO: On being told that a friend was pregnant, the American wit Dorothy Parker sent a telegram saying, 'Congratulations. We knew you had it in you.' Leos love to get straight to the point.

VIRGO: When he heard that his son was going to be married, Virgo Sam Goldwyn said, 'Thank God! A bachelor's life is no life for a single man.' He also said, 'Anyone who needs to see a psychiatrist needs his head examined.' Virgos can even use meaningless words convincingly in conversation.

LIBRA: Sylvia Kristel has often been heard to say, 'Yes . . . yes . . . oh, yes, yes . . . yes . . .'

4

Librans can be very obliging. And very sharp. Witness Libran Oscar Wilde's remark when a critic said, 'Oscar, I passed your house yesterday.' 'Thank you,' said Oscar.

SCORPIO: Bill Wyman was once rumoured to have said, 'You know the difference between me and a greyhound, darlin'? Greyhounds wait for the hare to come out first . . . '
Scorpios are generally strange and always sex-mad.

SAGITTARIUS: Typically paranoid Sagittarius Woody Allen admitted that his brother thought he was a chicken. 'Then why don't you send him to the funny farm?' asked a friend. 'I would,' said Woody, 'but we need the eggs.'

CAPRICORN: Comedienne Joan Rivers says a girl should never admit to being older than her bra size. It's hard to believe Miss Rivers is only 6! Maybe we shouldn't believe all that stuff astrologers say about Capricorn girls growing old gracefully.

AQUARIUS: The typical male Aquarian attitude to women is best summed up by Aquarian Clark Gable's 'Frankly, my dear, I don't give a damn.' This philosophy also seems to have affected fellow star-sign John McEnroe's tennis and Ronnie Reagan's foreign policy. Though there was one considerably more refined Aquarian (a very long time ago), Charles Dickens. When a poet sent him a tediously long piece titled 'Orient Pearls at Random Strung', Dickens simply replied, 'Dear Author, Too much string. Yours, C.D.'

PISCES: Like Pisces people, Pisces sayings are always weird. They range from Samuel Pepys's, 'My wife has something in her gizzard!' to Prince Edward's, 'I don't want to play soldiers anymore, Mummy' to Philip Roth saying, 'Since I was a little girl I always wanted to be very decent to people.' But, like Patrick Moore, most Pisces think astrology's a load of old cod – well, they have to, don't they?

5

Aries

THE SIGN OF THE RAMPANT

March 21st – April 20th

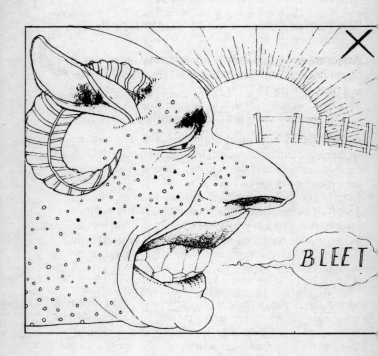

BLEET

6

The first Fire sign – and therefore permanently on heat.

Arietians are frequently – adventurous, assertive, active, arsonists, arseholes.

Some famous Rams – Rambo, Brando, Casanova, Samantha Fox, Leonardo, Jeffrey Archer, Ali MacGraw, Julie Christie, most of the patients in *One Flew Over the Cuckoo's Nest*.

Typical occupations – sheepshagger, mercenary, Mafia boss, dentist, person who puts the wiggly bits on chocolates.

Greatest failing – being the first sign of the entire zodiac, they need to be put first in everything.

Greatest problem – all Aries have incredibly whiffy armpits.

The saddest Aries ever – Dudley Moore's father – the man whose prayers were slightly misheard . . . God gave him a twelve-inch pianist.

ARIES AND SEX

They're either as fiery as that old Ram, Casanova, or else they're like Neil Kinnock, who has trouble getting an election . . .

ARIES WITH A MUSICAL EAR . . .

Diana Ross, Billie Holliday, Aretha Franklin, J. S. Bach, Andrew Lloyds-Bank, Stephen Sondheim, Elton John, Toscanini, Haydn, André Previn, James Last.

ARIES WITHOUT . . .

Vincent Van Gogh.

ARIES AND FELLATIO

The only thing that really went down in style under Aries was the Titanic, which sank on April 15th. Otherwise this old Aries conversation says it all . . . *Aries Woman*: 'If you were a gentleman, you wouldn't make me do this . . .' *Aries Man*: 'If you were a lady, you wouldn't speak with your mouth full . . .' (N.B. Aries men are seldom this subtle.)

ARIES IN BUSINESS

If anyone's going to fleece you, it's the Ram. Like Aries Lucrezia Borgia, they can be bloody cut-throat. Like Jeffrey Archer, they adore machinations, and having several strings to their bow. But they *can* be too clever for their own good . . . remember how Aries Michael Heseltine came under the chopper . . .

FAVE CAR

Anything phallus-shaped, ideally an E-type. Remember, these men don't have balls, they have furry dice.

LEO SHOCK

Why can you never hear what Leos are saying when they're sitting down?

BLACK SHEEP

There's an old story about an Aries tribal leader who was particularly distraught when one of his flock of black wives gave birth to a white baby. He sought solace from the local Christian missionary, who simply pointed to a black sheep amongst a flock of white ones. In typical Aries style, the complete dickhead of a chieftain entirely missed the point and whispered, 'I no tell if you no tell.'

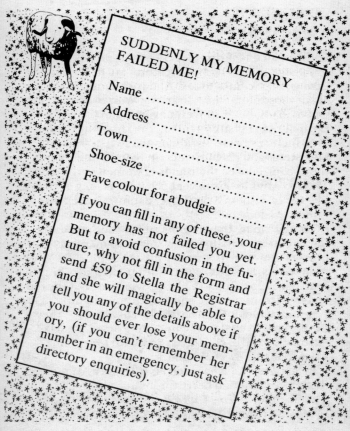

SUDDENLY MY MEMORY FAILED ME!

Name ....

Address ....

Town ....

Shoe-size ....

Fave colour for a budgie ....

If you can fill in any of these, your memory has not failed you yet. But to avoid confusion in the future, why not fill in the form and send £59 to Stella the Registrar and she will magically be able to tell you any of the details above if you should ever lose your memory, (if you can't remember her number in an emergency, just ask directory enquiries).

ARIES MAN

Randy is an understatement. These typically impulsive and passionate creatures are never more so than when it comes to sex. And we're not just talking about those old Rams: Casanova, Warren Beatty and Omar Sharif, but also Werner von Braun (inventor of the first flying phallic symbol, the Dildobug). Aries even includes those world-famous swingers Sevvy Ballesteros and Hugh Hefner. In their various ways, they've introduced thousands of women to the club. Though Aries lovers never keep it up as long as they'd like to . . . witness Aries Roger Bannister, the four-minute-male.

To Aries man, the male member is nothing other than a battering Ram, which is why so many of these hearty fellows are frequently mistaken for Australians. In true Ozzie tradition, their idea of true romance is going up to a Sheila, whipping out the old one-eyed trouser snake and saying quite bluntly, 'Do you wanna fuck?' On hearing the answer 'No', they simply say, 'Well do you mind lying down while I have one?' And during the act, as with everything, Aries man just *has* to be on top.

In fact, Australia has seen far too many Aries men. Remember Arietian heart-throb Richard Chamberlain in *The Thorn Birds*? It wasn't a thorn that caused problems was it? It was a prick.

Nevertheless, nobody can deny that Aries is the sign of an incredibly big prick . . . Norman Tebbit. Arietians even include Britain's biggest Willy in history – Willy Wordsworth, who, in true Aries style, wandered lonely as a clot, bonking anything in sight . . . including his poor sister Dorothy. In fact, the supposedly Wordsworthian philosophy of 'Pantheism', where the believer sees spiritual life throughout the landscape is, in fact, simply a mis-spelling of the Arietian philosophy 'Panty-ism', where the landscape is littered with pairs of panties the old Ram has ripped off during his many conquests. And if anyone's into quantity – in passion, power, possessions, whatever – it's Aries. In bed especially. They never settle down while there's still a chance of a rampage. They can't resist the thrill of the chaste. Look at Casanova and Warren Beatty. As far as any Ram goes, bed's never a place for sleep, it's a place for counting sheep . . .

POLITICS SHOCK

Did you know that Nancy Reagan shares a birthday with her husband's main adviser, Sylvester Stallone? (See under Cancerians with Lobotomies.)

ARIES WOMAN

Just as Aries man is so often the hearty rugby type, Aries woman can be equally happy as a hooker playing the field. Don't forget that this is the sign of Bet Lynch and that famous Hussey, Olivia, both of whom would do anything for a Romeo.

But for one or two kinky exceptions, you'll rarely find an Aries woman that likes being tied down. Bondage is definitely something female Rams get sheepish about. No, this is the sign of some very independent ladies, notably the first female pirate, *Radio Caroline*, born under Aries. Also at sea and just as independent, Clare Francis who, unlike Aries men, knows that you don't have to be Jewish to undergo circumnavigation. But although they're very organised and ship-shape, Aries girls are hardly what you'd call Bristol-fashion. With few exceptions they are flat-chested and skinny. The exception being Sam Fox, who makes up for all Aries women in history put together. Still, if they don't make the upper bust, Aries women certainly include plenty of upper crust. Remember, this is the first sign of the zodiac, the ones that want everything to the manor born, like Aries Penelope Keith. And just like Aries men, you'll find plenty of big knobs in the magazine that was born under Aries, *The Tatler*. Likewise, the knobby TV channel born under Aries, BBC 2.

Of course the downside of this superior sign is that they are all incredibly impatient. The only Aries woman that's been famous for waiting is Diana Ross. Otherwise, be late for a date with Miss Aries and your bird will have flown. In virtually every relationship, Aries woman likes to call the tune. The only exceptions are those where she doesn't like to call the tune. Maybe that's why they make such successful solo singers. Diana Ross, Billie Holliday, Sam Fox (though she's really a double-act), Aretha Franklyn and Dusty Springfield, who was always equally black round the eyes, and always being invited to sit down and take the weight off her mascara.

Aries women can certainly be extravagant. And they won't accept second best. In older years, this can easily lead to mutton dressing as lamb, Bet Lynch style, but they won't take criticism easily. A positive Aries lady will be determined to prove she can be just as frisky as a young lamb, whatever her age. And who's going to argue with the sign of Joan Crawford? She could certainly put away the Lamb's.

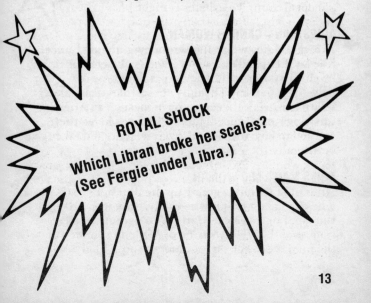

ROYAL SHOCK

Which Libran broke her scales?
(See Fergie under Libra.)

13

ARIES MAN – ARIES WOMAN

Fire sign with fire sign, like those old flames Warren Beatty and Julie Christie. The trouble with this is that, both partners being the type to burn the candle at both ends, the relationship soon burns itself out too. There's nothing left to discover. Sooner or later a Ram surrounded by other sheep is bound to say, 'I'm getting the flock out of here and finding someone less demanding.'

ARIES MAN – TAURUS WOMAN

They may see eye to eye over some things . . . take Aries Dudley Moore with Her Taurean Majesty the Queen; both leave the country short . . . but this can never be a successful relationship once it goes beyond the platonic. Taurean Florence Nightingale might have been excellent with men in bed, but randy Aries would be wounded if she refused to dress up in a nurse's outfit for all sorts of other reasons!

ARIES MAN – GEMINI WOMAN

(Under Gemini. Especially at night.)

ARIES MAN – CANCER WOMAN

Arrogant Aries won't like a money-grabbing Cancer like Lady Di, and she won't like his always wanting to be put first; nor will the even crabbier type of Cancer lady, Sybil Fawlty. The only succesful Aries/Cancer relationship is between some men, such as Aries Casanova and Cancer Henry VIII: both loved their women to give them head, even if Henry did take it a bit literally . . .

ARIES MAN – LEO WOMAN

Aries man will hate giving up the limelight to those who depend on it, but who can out-fox women with the same sign as Mata Hari? Who's going to tell a lioness of the Helen Mirren or Madonna variety that the man should be on top? No, the only likely Aries/

Leo link is between those with an artistic bent (bent being the operative word) like Leo Danny la Rue and Aries Hans Christian Andersen, both full of fairy stories . . .

ARIES MAN – VIRGO WOMAN

Nobody can deny that a so-called Virgo like 'Sue Ellen' wouldn't be attracted by a Ram, but these Cow girls love anything horny. But the average Ram's idea of sheer enjoyment would lack all the intellectual stimulation Virgo women need . . . after all, Virgos have got such a lot up top . . . just look at Raquel Welch and Sophia Loren.

ARIES MAN – LIBRA WOMAN

Remember that Libra is the sign of some of history's most famous humpers, namely Richard III and Sylvia Kristel. Her idea of balance is simply having one on each end. Such a Libral attitude towards giving everyone their fair share isn't going to please the man who likes to be made to feel important. Otherwise, it's Libran Maggie Thatcher versus Aries Neil Kinnock. And, in a confrontation, could he honestly keep his hair on?

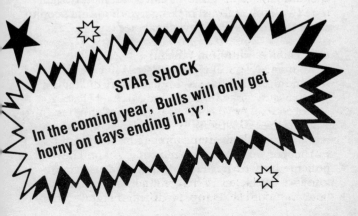

STAR SHOCK

In the coming year, Bulls will only get horny on days ending in 'Y'.

ARIES MAN – SCORPIO WOMAN

Sexually speaking, the fiery Ram is bound to go for the sign of 'Hotlips' from M.A.S.H. and Goldie Hawn. Otherwise, she's far too explosive, far too jealous for such a fickle creature as Aries to cope with. Remember Rams need new conquests constantly; for them, bed's a place for counting sheep . . .

ARIES MAN – SAGITTARIUS WOMAN

A Sagittarian dame like Bette Midler or Pamela Stephenson will instantly appeal as 'one of the lads' whose company heartier Aries will enjoy, but outside the pub these fire signs will burn themselves out if either one tries to order the other about. They'll be great sports until old Aries realises she can keep up with him. Best match: Aries man with a Sagittarian type like Madame Tussaud or Bo Derek. Aries man loves to think of women as dummies.

ARIES MAN – CAPRICORN WOMAN

Well, the Rod Steiger type of Aries could get on well with an old goat like Princess Michael . . . both advanced their careers considerably 'in the heat of the night', but while the Ram's never sheepish about spending sprees, Capricorns can be incredibly tight-fisted . . . look at Jesus, making five thousand people share two loaves and five fishes.

ARIES MAN – AQUARIUS WOMAN

Aries men always like a good joke. After all, they include all those famous clowns, Charlie Chaplin, Chico Marx, Spike Milligan and Michael Heseltine – and of course, April Fool's Day falls under Aries. But Aquarians like Germaine Greer, Vanessa Redgrave and Virginia Woolf aren't going to be at all impressed by that old wolf in sheep's clothing, Aries. They prefer to bury themselves in books and everyone knows Arietians can't read. Aquarius women will pour water on all his fire, producing a real wet blanket.

ARIES MAN – PISCES WOMAN

Randy Rams are bound to go for women in fish-nets, but her romantic dreams will be shattered by his bonk-a-minute physicality. Fish people prefer to think about things rather than do them. Aries prefer to do people and not have to think about it. Aries man likes things basic, none of the song and dance that goes with Fish like Liza Minnelli, Nina Simone or Vera Lynn. And they certainly can't handle Fish like Liz Taylor, who can't survive unless surrounded by liquid . . .

FUTURE FORECAST

In the coming year, all Aries will continue to wander around fruit and vegetable stalls proclaiming, 'Mine's bigger than that!'

WHAT DO YOU SHARE

BORN

MARCH 21st Michael Heseltine, Johann Sebastian Bach.

MARCH 22nd Andrew-Lloyds Bank, Stephen Sondheim, Leslie Thomas, George Benson.

MARCH 23rd Roger Bannister, Werner Von Braun (inventor of the flying phallic symbol), Chaka Khan.

MARCH 24th Malcolm Muggeridge, William Morris.

MARCH 25th Aretha Franklin, Elton John, David Lean, Arturo Toscanini.

MARCH 26th Leonard Nimoy ('Mr Spock'), Diana Ross, Chico Marx.

MARCH 27th Michael York, Jim Callaghan.

MARCH 28th Dirk Bogarde, Neil Kinnock, Michael Parkinson.

MARCH 29th Eric Idle, The even more idle Norman Tebbit, Radio Caroline, Julie Goodyear, 'Bet Lynch'.

MARCH 30th Warren Beatty, Eric Clapton, Rolf Harris, Goya, Vincent Van Gogh.

MARCH 31st Richard Chamberlain, David Steel, Haydn, John Fowles.

APRIL 1st Ali MacGraw and that fool Bismarck. Marvin Gaye died.

APRIL 2nd Paul Gambaccini, Sir Alec Guinness, Penelope Keith, Casanova, Emil Zola, Hans Christian Andersen, Marvin Gaye.

APRIL 3rd Marlon Brando, Doris Day, Tony Benn.

APRIL 4th Anthony Perkins (from *Psycho* – one of the saner Aries).

APRIL 5th Jane Asher, Gregory Peck, Arthur Hailey.

APRIL 6th Ian Paisley, Paul Daniels, Houdini, Raphael, André Previn.

WITH THESE RAMS?

APRIL 7th	Francis Ford Coppola, Billie Holliday, William Wordsworth, David Frost, Andrew 'Manuel' Sachs.
APRIL 8th	Eric Porter, Alfie Bass.
APRIL 9th	Severiano Ballesteros, Hugh Hefner, McDonalds (1955).
APRIL 10th	Omar Sharif.
APRIL 11th	Nobody interesting at all.
APRIL 12th	David Cassidy, Alan Ayckbourn, *The Tatler*.
APRIL 13th	'Clayton' from *Dallas*, Samuel Beckett, John Braine, Thomas Jefferson.
APRIL 14th	Julie Christie, John Gielgud, Rod Steiger.
APRIL 15th	Samantha Fox, and the man who had even bigger boobs in the papers, Jeffrey Archer, also Leonardo Da Vinci and Claudia Cardinale.
APRIL 16th	Spike Milligan, Joan Bakewell, Dusty Springfield, Charlie Chaplin, Peter Ustinov.
APRIL 17th	Clare Francis, Kruschev.
APRIL 18th	Lucrezia Borgia, *Dynasty* star, John James.
APRIL 19th	Dudley Moore, The first Miss World contest, Alan Price.
APRIL 20th	Ryan O'Neal, BBC 2, Luther Vandross, Nicholas Lyndhurst.

Nobody will admit to Adolf Hitler being on their birthday, but it's on the cusp with Taurus, so almost definitely April 20th. All Aries claim he's a Bull, all Bulls claim he was an Aries, certainly an Arian.

Taurus

HER MAJESTY THE QUEEN

12ᵖ

BY APPOINTMENT

TAURUS

SIGN OF THE BULLSHITTER

APRIL 21st – MAY 21st

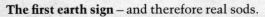

The first earth sign – and therefore real sods.

Taureans are frequently – bullish, basic, stubborn, greedy, miserly, plodding, possessive, fat.

Ruler – The Queen.

Some famous Bulls – Sitting Bull, Sigmund Freud, Charlotte Brontë, Grace Jones, Denis Thatcher, Adolf Hitler, 'Dirty Den' and 'Angie' from *EastEnders*.

Typical occupations – Traffic warden, milkman, Fascist dictator (in which case occupations include France, Holland, Belgium and anything else you can get your Hans on!).

Only good point – Taureans can make great singers . . . Streisand, Ella Fitzgerald, Stevie Wonder, Irving Berlin.

Fave song – What else for Mr Berlin and Adolf . . . it's 'Knees up, Eva Braun.'

Famous Taurean Queens – Queen Elizabeth II, Liberace, Gary Glitter, Jeremy Thorpe.

Most compatible sign – pub sign.

Favourite hobbies – performing post-mortems on the contents of their handkerchiefs (whereas Sagittarians simply treat these as free snacks). Plucking nasal hairs at traffic lights.

TAURUS AND SEX

Sexually speaking, typical Taureans have all the appeal of a grandfather-clock. They may be big, they may stand erect, but they've got incredibly predictable hand movements, faces we've all seen before and thoroughly wooden bodies. This is not to say that Bulls don't like a bit of the udder. As Earth signs, they delight in earthy pleasures. It's just that Taureans are incredibly unadventurous. Foreplay? Never heard of it! Mixed Doubles? They still think it's something to do with tennis! Routine? Now that's the Taurean idea of having a good time!

TAURUS AND MULTIPLE ORGASM

TAURUS AND FASHION

This is the green welly brigade. As far as Taurus goes, if they've seen it on farmers, it's fashionable! So their fave boutique is *Millets*. Their favourite headgear is a flat cap, the perfect fit for the Taurean brain. One or two Taureans also sport armbands and the odd jackboot.

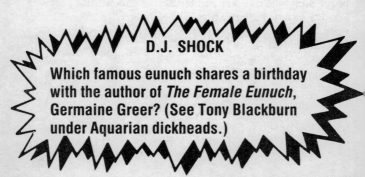

D.J. SHOCK

Which famous eunuch shares a birthday with the author of *The Female Eunuch*, Germaine Greer? (See Tony Blackburn under Aquarian dickheads.)

TAUREANS DRIVE . . .

Rovers, Volvos and anyone with a sense of adventure round the bend.

ON FIRST IMPRESSIONS . . .

Positive Taureans come across as non-stop Bullshitters. Negative ones appear the strong, silent type. This is simply because they have difficulty in pronouncing most words.

TAURUS MAN

How well do you know your Taurus man? 1. Do you know his name? 2. Do you know his star-sign? 3. Has he introduced you to anything other than the missionary position?

If you answered 'Yes' to Question 3, he's lying about being a Taurean. You see, there's a very good reason why they put bulls in fields by themselves; they can bore every other animal rigid. With all the fashion sense and sex appeal of Ken Barlowe, the average Bull would always swap a Club 18–30 beach bonking party for a chance to take the local Boy Scouts on a field trip. Somewhere where he can air his rigid views to people too young to realise that he's just talking a load of his own sign.

Physically, the male of the species often has a thick neck and an even thicker head, and his vast appetite for truckloads of home-cooking soon makes him as rotund as that old Bull, Orson Welles. They're also very big drinkers, look at Albert Finney or Denis Thatcher (though who can blame him?), and possibly

23

as a result, their apparently warm manner and broody eyes can quickly burst into something explosive and evil. Note James Mason, Jack Nicholson and old Adolf.

Politically, they are either just a few goose-steps to the right of Genghis Khan, or otherwise, negative bullshitters, like Karl Marx. Either way, they're stubborn as hell. ('Dirty Den' would claim he's not stubborn, just permanently rigid.)

Taureans nearly always have dark hair, unless they are blond, and they are always most at home in their own houses, where their idea of slipping into something positively daring is walking round in Hush Puppies instead of carpet slippers.

TAURUS WOMAN

One famous astrologer wrote in all seriousness that the Taurean woman 'is not depressed or worried if her partner only has the IQ of a retarded ant.' This is clearly borne out when you realise that the Queen is a Taurean. The perfect farmer's wife, she is happiest at home, surrounded by home-grown vegetables. No doubt this is why Her Majesty keeps so many relatives at the palace.

Taureans hate change. They far prefer notes. Once again, like Her Royal Highness, they need to feel comfortably off without ever having to exert themselves and the thrifty Taurean mother can *easily* get by on the five or six million a year housekeeping money she has come to expect. The landed gentry make great Taureans . . . especially where fashion is concerned, because this is the Green Welly Brigade. Strapping, unfeminine country gels, or Earth Mothers in smocks and support socks. Talk about intriguing underwear and they think you mean sewn-in groundsheets. They build warm, cosy homes, serve rich, red wines like Bull's Blood and enjoy the slapstick humour of Taurean Terry Scott. Victoria Wood is simply Taurean in shape. The rest of these stupid old moos are about as sophisticated as *Emmerdale Farm*, (Her Majesty's favourite programme).

STAR SHOCK

Who is living proof that Pisces have to be surrounded by liquid? (See Liz Taylor under Drinking like a Fish.)

THE TAURUS CHILD

With very few exceptions, the Taurus child is nearly always a little Taurus man or a little Taurus woman.

STAR SHOCK
Which outstanding debs share the same birthday, July 1st? (See under Cancer.)

SEX SHOCK
Which DIY enthusiasts really believe you can't have a good screw without first inserting a rawl plug? (See Libra and dubious habits.)

TAURUS MAN – ARIES WOMAN

Can you really see fiery Arietian women like Grace Jones or Julie Mitchell being anything other than frustrated by plodding Taureans like weatherman Michael Fish or the permanently inebriated Denis Thatcher? She's far too much a doer, far too impulsive – he's far too much an observer and far too repulsive. No, the only successful Taurus/Aries match is in business . . . the Hitler/Houdini relationship where, however much trouble the first one gets into, the second always finds a way out.

TAURUS MAN – TAURUS WOMAN

Mr and Mrs Moderation. One bonk a month, 2–3 children and a Labrador in the back of the Volvo Estate. They never read thrillers, they prefer guidebooks. (Many of them can't read.) At heart, they are simple country folk. In America they are Glen Campbell and Tammy Wynette; in England, the Queen in unfeminine tweeds and a Barbour, with Lord Letchfield in predictable Burberry or David Attenborough in sensible safari shirt. Their idea of doing something daring is planting next year's vegetables a week earlier than it says on the seed packet. Happy together until somebody wants a change of routine.

TAURUS MAN – GEMINI WOMAN

Unlike changeable Gemini, every Bull adores routine. He likes everything he will do next year to be perfectly fitting with everything he does this year. While Gemini girls ask for gems, Taureans are the men who actually request socks for Christmas. While Gemini Joan Collins will want *Dynasty* style gowns, Taurus man will want matching sheepskin jackets and walking boots. The only possible outcome . . . she'll tell him to take a hike.

TAURUS MAN – CANCER WOMAN

Not a bad match. The Bull and the Crab have a mutual love of creature comforts. Both enjoy being pampered, though a Cancerian like Lady Di can take it too far. Unless she finds a rich Taurean like the *Six-Million Dollar Man*, Lee Majors, her seven figure clothing allowance will set most Bulls raging. Still, Taurean Sloanes like Lady Sarah Armstrong-Jones and Lady Helen 'Melons' Windsor will understand her pratty accent.

TAURUS MAN – LEO WOMAN

Taureans will never be lion-tamers. In fact those over-indulgent lusty Leos are practically untameable. They include Mata Hari, Madonna and Princess Margaret. While Taureans love home, Leos love to roam. The only happy Bull with this lot would be a green welly wally like Lord Letchfield. In fact, Taureans and Leos make great royals . . . neither minds how much anything costs provided somebody else is paying.

TAURUS MAN – VIRGO WOMAN

While Taurus men like 'Dirty Den' can be unbearably basic, with all the manners of a farm animal, Virgo women have got a lot up top . . . look at Raquel Welch and Sophia Loren, both with a good pair of 'A' levels, (or is it 'eye-levels' . . . ?) And the typical Virgo will hate the Bull's vast appetite. Remember Virgos are health-freaks and pessimists . . . the people who put prunes on their muesli!

TAURUS MAN – LIBRA WOMAN

Both ruled by Venus, these two find each other instantly attractive. Take Taurus Adolf Hitler with Libran Maggie Thatcher. Could there ever be a more compatible pair? For the more easy-going, both signs can enjoy that famous Taurus/Libra partnership so frequently enjoyed by Mr Thatcher/Brahms and Liszt.

TAURUS MAN – SCORPIO WOMAN

Methodical Bulls like Oliver Cromwell cannot accept the cavalier spirit of Scorpios like Goldie Hawn. And civil war is what any Taurus/Scorpio marriage will become. Witness Taurean Terry Scott with Scorpio June Whitfield. Though *Terry and June* could do with a few real stings in the tail; perhaps that would convince viewers that it was supposed to be a comedy, not a documentary on the living dead.

TAURUS MAN – SAGITTARIUS WOMAN

Can you really see a conventional Bull like Bing Crosby surviving the animal passion of a Sagittarian like Tina Turner? Imagine the duet . . . 'I'm screaming of a white Christmas, with split-crutch panties and leather bras . . .' Or could that old Bull from the ring really go the distance with Bette Midler or Pamela Stephenson? No, the only Taurus/Sagbag relationship with anything in common would have been Orson Welles with Bo Derek . . . neither could remember ever seeing their feet.

TAURUS MAN – CAPRICORN WOMAN

It's easy to see why Capricorns aren't interested in anything bovine. Just picture that famous goat Joan of Arc being asked if she'd fancy a steak. No, a stubborn Bull would never make sacrifices to the martyr in Capricorn. Mind you, a Capricorn like Princess Michael might well find something to talk about to a belligerent Bull like Adolf . . .

CAPRICORN SHOCK

Do you realise that most of Capricorn is apric?

✸ TAURUS MAN – AQUARIUS WOMAN

In Taurus/Aquarian documentaries you'd see David Attenborough coming up against that weird species Germaine Greer. In TV comedy you'd see the ever ebullient Victoria Wood versus the warped Benny Hill. Next to those loveable Bulls, Aquarians are either fanatical, eccentric or just plain perverted and they are always leading others astray. Witness, Water-bearer and all-barer Nell Gwynne, peeling off for a king and taking the pith out of the queen . . .

✸ TAURUS MAN – PISCES WOMAN

These two signs could get along extremely well, provided neither showed any of their typical star-sign characteristics. Conservative in bed as everywhere, Bulls won't allow dreamy Pisceans their fantasies . . . fish-nets, codpieces, soft-prawn . . . Is a Piscean like Liza Minnelli really going to get hooked by a Taurean like Michael Fish? No, Pisceans need hidden depths to explore. The Taurus/Pisces forecast looks gloomy.

POLITICS SHOCK

Which female British Prime Minister was born on the same day as Damien Omen, Attila the Hun and the lead in *Alien*?

FUTURE FORECAST

In the coming year, Bulls will only get horny on days ending in 'Y'.

STAR SHOCK

The Twins are not necessarily schizophrenic. Ask Geminis Prince Philip or the Duke of Edinburgh.

NATURE SHOCK

How many pea-brained molluscs have been reincarnated as American presidents? (See Reagan under Aquarius.)

STAR SHOCK

The knack for coming out with the perfect answer when put on the spot is a trait of many Geminis. For instance, when asked, 'Ten pence for a cup of tea, Guv?' typical Geminis will answer, quite shrewdly, 'Fuck off!'

ARE YOU AS BULLISH

BORN

APRIL 21st	The Queen, Charlotte Brontë, John Mortimer, Anthony Quinn, Iggy Pop. (Adolf Hitler, on the cusp with Aries, also raised his ugly head this day).
APRIL 22nd	Peter Frampton, Glenn Campbell, Yehudi Menuhin, George Cole ('Arfur Daley').
APRIL 23rd	Lee Majors, Roy Orbison, William Shakespeare, J. M. W. Turner.
APRIL 24th	Shirley Maclaine, Barbra Streisand, John Williams.
APRIL 25th	Sitting Bull, Ella Fitzgerald, Patrick Litchfield, Oliver Cromwell.
APRIL 26th	Duane Eddy.
APRIL 27th	Michael Fish (who predicted his own birth as gloomy).
APRIL 28th	Jack Nicholson, Ann-Margret, Lady Helen 'Melons' Windsor.
APRIL 29th	Jeremy 'More Thrust, Scottie' Thorpe, Duke Ellington, similarly famous for band (or was it banned) members . . . Anita Dobson ('Angie' from *Eastenders*).
APRIL 30th	Dirty Den, Jill Clayburgh, Dickie Davies.
MAY 1st	Joanna Lumley, Joseph Heller, Lady Sarah Armstrong-Jones.
MAY 2nd	Bianca Jagger, Bing Crosby, Dr Spock the child-care man, Englebert Humperdinck.
MAY 3rd	Machiavelli, Henry Cooper, Patti Boulaye.

AS THIS LOT?

MAY 4th	Audrey Hepburn, Tammy Wynette, The Epsom Derby.
MAY 5th	Karl Marx, Michael Palin, Dr Hugh Jolly.
MAY 6th	Orson Welles, Sigmund Freud, Robespierre, Valentino, the Penny Black.
MAY 7th	Eva Peron, Robert Browning, Johannes Brahms.
MAY 8th	David Attenborough, and that weird species Gary Glitter.
MAY 9th	Candice Bergen, Alan Bennett, Albert Finney, Glenda Jackson, Billy Joel.
MAY 10th	Denis Thatcher, Donovan, Fred Astaire is born.
MAY 11th	Phil Silvers, Salvador Dali, Irving Berlin.
MAY 12th	Burt Bacharach, Florence Nightingale, Alcoholics Anonymous.
MAY 13th	Stevie Wonder, Selina Scott.
MAY 14th	Thomas Gainsborough, Sian Phillips, David Byrne (Talking Heads).
MAY 15th	James Mason, Anthony Shaffer, Peter Shaffer, Ralph Steadman.
MAY 16th	Liberace, Roy Hudd, the Hollywood Oscar, Janet Jackson.
MAY 17th	Dennis Potter, Grace Jones, Ayatollah Khomeini.
MAY 18th	Toyah Wilcox, Perry Como, Fred Perry, Bertrand Russell.
MAY 19th	Victoria Wood, Pete Townshend, Philip Michael Thomas, Grace Jones.
MAY 20th	Cher, James Stewart, Honoré de Balzac.
MAY 21st	Harold Robbins, Raymund Burr, Albrecht Dürer.

Gemini

SIGN OF THE TWO-FACED BASTARD
MAY 22nd – JUNE 21st

The first air sign – and therefore love to give themselves airs, as does Gemini Prince Philip.

Twins are frequently – boys or girls.

Words often associated with Gemini – Geminis, two-timing, restless, unrelaxed, gender-bender, bigamy, bugger me!

Famous Gemini Queens – Victoria, Boy George, George III, Prince.

Other famous Twins – The Thomson Twins, the Cocteau Twins, Jekyll and Hyde, Joan Collins, Paul McCartney, Paul Weller, Clint Eastwood, and 'Pinky and Perky', (as Joan calls her twin appendages).

Fave sign – two fingers to anyone who doesn't agree with them.

Overall impression – because these restless creatures can never stay in one place, they are often referred to as the 'butterflies' of the zodiac, though a Gemini like Enoch Powell would hate to think that he was related to a cocoon.

Greatest failing – the Twins should really be known as the Twits. Look at Prince Philip . . . though Geminis love to pontificate and display their characteristic little learning about a lot of things, underneath it all, they're pillocks.

Fave transport – tandem (Just like Joan, they love 'riding two-up').

Typical Gemini jobs – impressionist (like Gemini Mike Yarwood), Ear Nose & Deep Throat Specialist (dear old Joan . . .), Pus remover in beauty parlour.

GEMINI AND SEX

As their symbol suggests, sex with a Gemini is like having a threesome. Totally unable to ever stay still, they really will give you the feeling that they've got two extra pairs of hands and legs and one extra everything else. It's never foreplay, it's eightplay! Their favourite sexual position . . . 696!

GEMINI AND MARZIPAN

Geminis do not like marzipan. But they do like the icing on the cake (Gemini women adore sugar daddies).

GEMINIS AND FASHION

For the women: twin-sets.
For the men: Double-breasted suits and twopés.

LIBRA SHOCK

Why do Libra women always get the better of Cancerians? (See Thatcher and Crushed Asians.)

GEMINIS AND NERVOUS COMPLAINTS

(Being published as a separate book . . . in twenty-four volumes).

GREATEST PROBLEM

Coping with their bi-sexuality. Wasn't it Boy George who said, 'I'm a bi-sexual . . . if I want sex, I have to buy it'?

FAVE BOOK

'Twice is not enough.'

FAVE FRUIT

Pears.

36

GEMINI MAN

They're not just two-faced, they're plain schizophrenic. Ask Prince Philip or the Duke of Edinburgh, to name but two. Like every Gemini, Gemini men are full of contradictions. Even two Geminis with exactly the same birthday can be totally different. Take James Bolam and Enoch Powell, both born on June 16th. The first is relaxed and easy-going 'when the boat comes in'; the second is terrified that there might be wogs in it when it arrives. And what greater contradiction could there be than that old two-timing stud – Tony Curtis – born on the birthday of *No Sex Please, We're British* . . .

In fact the theatre has seen many Geminis. They adore playing and story-telling. They love pretending to be somebody important . . . just look at Mike Yarwood and Prince Philip. Other Gemini actors include Larry Olivier, Rupert Everett, Malcolm McDowell, Peter Cushing and Vincent Price; the last three displaying the characteristic Gemini fascination with the weird and the macabre. Remember the Marquis de Sade was not in fact a black singer's tent, but something even darker. In fact, Gemini men have inflicted a great deal of pain on other people . . . Barry Manilow . . . Burl Ives . . . On the pain stakes, don't forget that the French reign of terror was born under Gemini. And Gemini man is at his most painful when he indulges in his favourite sport – flirting. It's all part of the acting; being one thing one minute, one thing the next; the reason why Geminis are all so incredibly hard to tie down.

Obvious exceptions being Ian Fleming and the Marquis de Sade, who were both into Bondage in a big way.

Otherwise, they are continually blowing hot and cold. Even the sportsmen. Take George Best and tennis ace Borg, also Björn under Gemini . . . both could be ice-cool during the game, but fiery in their private lives. Mind you, all their opponents admitted that playing against these two was like facing two ordinary players . . . but every now and then there's a Gemini who's twice as good as a single human. But it's rare. As a rule, they are weak-willed, nervy chain-smokers. That's the typical negative Gemini, the dandy who gets through hundreds of fags: Boy George, Beau Brummell and George III are typical Gemini fops. John Wayne and Clint Eastwood are not, which just goes to show that astrology's a load of bollocks. Or maybe, they're just the positive Geminis, the swashbuckling brigade, the true grit cowboys who are all convinced that where real men are real men, Geminis are twice as big as anyone else. Well, who can argue with Gemini Errol Flynn? Didn't he prove that 'the penis mightier than the sword'?

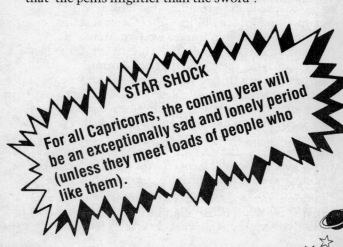

STAR SHOCK

For all Capricorns, the coming year will be an exceptionally sad and lonely period (unless they meet loads of people who like them).

GEMINI WOMAN

The Bitch. The two-timer. The gossip. The flirt. The kiss-and-tell actress. Assertive. Careerist yet fanciful. The only constant thing about a Gemini woman is her changeability. These are the girls who put the whim in women. Even though they get twice as much out of everything for themselves, to anyone else they're just double trouble.

Who could keep Gemini Queen Victoria amused? And she had even more people under her than Joan Collins. These women just *have* to be on top. Everywhere . . . and they do it by prick-teasing. Marilyn Monroe, Jane Russell, Joan, they're all Geminis. And people can tell instantly. The number of men who've looked at any one of these girls and immediately recognised the Gemini symbol with the phrase, 'What a pair!' And dealing with girls who can handle so many parts is always like dealing with two ordinary people. In business, in bed, wherever. However, Gemini women do very well for themselves, earning twice as much as other actresses, having twice as many husbands, two-timing wherever they please, leading double lives . . . and men just fall for it.

There are only two well-known Gemini women who *can't* get a man's rising sign into the ascendant . . . Moira Anderson and Mary Whitehouse (though she's only bored with sex because she's spent twice as long looking into it as anyone normal). And the fact that Mary Whitehouse shares the same sign as Marilyn Monroe is not such a typical Gemini contradiction anyway . . . both girls have climbed on top of the head of a White House at some time or other . . .

And the reason these girls get to the top is: they take a mile where others would accept an inch (in Joan's case, taking six miles where others would settle for six inches . . .). And if anyone's brave enough to challenge them, they simply play on his emotions. It is no coincidence that Joan of Arc was burned at the stake when the sun was in Gemini . . . this sign has given birth to more martyrs than any other.

Gemini women even annoy other women. Where normal signs settle down to a career or a family, these two-timers generally manage both. The only compensation is that all that extra living starts to show twice as soon, which is why so many of them wear make-up by Polyfilla. And why Gemini girls wear such provocative underwear . . . to divert you away from their faces. And they're twice as demanding in bed. Don't be fooled if they borrow Gemini Clint Eastwood's invitation, 'Go ahead . . . make my lay.' A Gemini woman in bed will demand twice the satisfaction, twice the number of orgasms . . . and she'll leave her lover, as Gemini comedian Mike Yarwood does, doubled up.

GEMINI MAN – ARIES WOMAN

Though Gemini Errol Flynn was famous for displaying the feature Aries men are most proud of, Gemini men are usually concerned with playing around with many other parts, like Laurence Olivier or Mike Yarwood. The impression one-track Aries gets is that her partner's being two-faced. She wants someone fixed, not restless. She wants the lust without the wander.

GEMINI MAN – TAURUS WOMAN

Prudish Taurus will never survive freedom-loving Gemini. Imagine Charlotte Brontë combining with Gemini Harold Robbins, *Jane Eyre* mixed up with *The Carpet-baggers*. Picture the scene where 'Randy' Rochester whips out his hot rod, unbuttons 'Juicy' Jane's nanny uniform and begs her to be his governess . . . No, for thrusting, forward-moving Geminis, Taureans like Selina Scott are yesterday's news.

GEMINI MAN – GEMINI WOMAN

Though many astrologers claim that a Gemini woman can make any man feel more of a man, remember that many astrologers are dickheads. I mean, could even Gemini Joan Collins do that for Gemini man Boy George? No, all they'd have in common is mascara, ballgowns and boyfriends.

Two may be company, but two Geminis is too much. Remember this is the Tony Curtis/Marilyn Monroe pairing; some find it too hot to handle. Imagine Gemini Wendy Craig with Gemini Errol Flynn . . . with a caterpillar like his she'd get butterflies constantly.

PISCES SHOCK

All Pisceans have had charisma by-pass operations at birth.

★ GEMINI MAN – CANCER WOMAN

On the whole, Gemini guys are pretty insecure and easily dominated by women. Take Joan Collins's last husband (this was written in Spring 1987, so I'm talking about the Scandinavian fellow. There could well have been several others since). Anyway, he will do no better up against crabby Cancerians like Prunella Scales or Esther Rantzen. He doesn't want anyone getting their claws into him. Like Gemini Clint Eastwood, he wants to be unattached, the man with no name. Though he might get on with Cancerian Nancy Reagan; she seems to like men who shoot first and ask questions later . . .

☆ GEMINI MAN – LEO WOMAN

A Gemini like Ken Livingstone is far too bright to chase the limelight the way most Leos do. He'll find it comes to him by keeping a low profile anyway. He won't agree to his lioness wanting the lion's share and singing in the reign like Leo Princess Margaret. No, the only Gemini her kind will feel akin to is Errol Flynn; both love being surrounded by big knobs of one sort or another . . .

★ GEMINI MAN – VIRGO WOMAN

Both ruled by Mercury, like thermometers, this couple will blow hot and cold, and it will be the Virgoan that decides. Take Agatha Christie and Sue Ellen, perfect proof that a Virgo girl can be calculating. They also tend to bend the truth somewhat. I mean, do you really believe Sue Ellen's claim to be a Virgo . . .?

MYSTIC DICK'S MESSAGES FROM THE OTHER WORLD

GEMINI MAN – LIBRA WOMAN

Red Ken and Maggie Thatcher? He may possess Gemini's versatility but he'll never accept a Libra who insists on balance even if it requires police enforcement. No, the only successful Gemini/Libra relationship is where his Mercurial rulings have made him so successful he can satisfy Libran lady's favourite balance – the one in the bank. Gemini man/Libra woman is the Paul McCartney/Linda McCartney relationship. Though just to show he's on top, Gemini man will always make his partner wear a ridiculously silly haircut.

☆☆

GEMINI MAN – SCORPIO WOMAN

It's no good a Gemini man like Errol Flynn thinking that Scorpio, the sign of Marie Antoinette, is going to let him have his cake and eat it. Not for long anyway; Scorpios are suspicious creatures. They may like the type of Gemini who, like Charles Saatchi and Cole Porter, can make money night and day but, being two creatures, Geminis always want everything else twice as big as well . . . Errol and his prick, Gemini Barry Manilow and his nose, Prince Philip with his bald patch. Why did Gemini Ian Fleming make James Bond a Scorpio? I don't know.

GEMINI MAN – SAGITTARIUS WOMAN

Old folks like Burl Ives would be eaten alive by outrageous Sagbags like Bette Midler; though young Gemini Boy George could share her passion for men. But he's an exception. Most Gemini men, like Paul McCartney, Cole Porter, Lionel Ritchie or Bob Dylan, may call a far less wild tune than Sagittarians like

CHULS OF WINDSOR – STOP TALKING TO VEGETABLES, ESPECIALLY YOUR FATHER.

Tina Turner, but they all know how to clean up. Clumsy Centaurs are just too impulsive. Quite apart from that, the Gemini love of detail would hate the fact that she rarely changes her underwear. (See under 'Sagittarius – dubious personal habits' for more details.)

 ### GEMINI MAN – CAPRICORN WOMAN
Unlike Gemini Boy George, Capricorns are typically unbending – the women anyway (more of David Bowie and Kenny Everett later). Being pretty self-centred, the Goats find it hard enough looking after their own careers . . . remember Janis Joplin? Coping with one partner is usually too much, but Twins? Like Victoria Principal, Capricorn women want a man who will help make 'them' big, and calculating Gemini will get fed up paying for all that silicone.

 ### GEMINI MAN – AQUARIUS WOMAN
Some say the flexible Aquarian is an ideal match for the many-sided Gemini. Others don't. Others say they both share a need for variety, so they quickly find new mates. Others say you can't generalise about people just because they're born at particular times of year. Bearing in mind that the Water-bearer is, in fact, not a Water but an Air sign, shows you just how wrong horoscopes can be. Still Geminis and Aquarians can have great relationships, provided they get on well together.

 ### GEMINI MAN – PISCES WOMAN
She'll find him far too dreary and down-to-earth. He'll find her far too dreamy and unable to keep her head above water. Still, a Gemini of the Dean Martin variety could well get on with a Liz Taylor type, the kind of Fish that needs to be permanently engulfed in liquid.

IN THE COMING YEAR . . .

Gemini drinkers will continue to say, 'Mine's a double!' (attributed to Gemini Dean Martin).

SPORTS SHOCK

Which tennis ace was born on the same day as the first Wimbledon final? (See July 19th under Cancer.)

WHAT DO YOU SHARE

BORN

MAY 22nd Jekyll & Hyde, Laurence Olivier, Sir Arthur Conan Doyle, George Best, Richard Wagner, Morrissey.

MAY 23rd Pinky & Perky, Joan Collins, John Newcombe, Humphrey Lyttleton.

MAY 24th Porgy & Bess, Queen Victoria, Bob Dylan, Stanley Baxter.

MAY 25th Dave Lee Travis, Lord Beaverbrook, Paul Weller.

MAY 26th John Wayne, Peter·Cushing, Matt Busby.

MAY 27th Vincent Price, the even more ghoulish Cilla Black, John Conteh and Herman Wouk.

MAY 28th Ian Fleming, Gladys Knight.

MAY 29th Rupert Everett, Nanette Newman, John F. Kennedy.

MAY 30th Ray Cooney, Joan of Arc burnt at stake.

MAY 31st Clint Eastwood, Prince Rainier, the French Reign of Terror began.

JUNE 1st Marilyn Monroe, Robert Powell, Bob Monkhouse, Nelson Riddle.

JUNE 2nd The Marquis de Sade, Charlie Watts, Elgar, Thomas Hardy.

JUNE 3rd Tony Curtis, *No Sex, Please, We're British*.

JUNE 4th Andrea Jaeger, George III (First Queen of Brighton).

WITH THESE TWINS?

JUNE 5th	Nigel Rees, Moira Anderson.
JUNE 6th	The day Borg was björn.
JUNE 7th	Tom Jones, Beau Bumhole, Paul Gaugin, Prince.
JUNE 8th	Nancy Sinatra, Frank Lloyd Wright, Nick Rhodes.
JUNE 9th	Charles Saatchi, Cole Porter.
JUNE 10th	Prince Philip, Robert Maxwell, First Oxford & Cambridge boat race.
JUNE 11th	Jacques Cousteau (inventor of the underwater bobble hat).
JUNE 12th	George Bush.
JUNE 13th	Mary Whitehouse, Malcolm McDowell.
JUNE 14th	Boy George, Mike Yarwood, Burl Ives, Julie Felix.
JUNE 15th	The Black Prince (the knight not the singer).
JUNE 16th	Enoch Powell, James Bolam.
JUNE 17th	Dean Martin, Ken Livingstone, Barry Manilow.
JUNE 18th	Paul McCartney, Ian Carmichael, Battle of Waterloo, Alison Moyet.
JUNE 19th	Salman Rushdie, Charlie Drake.
JUNE 20th	Errol Flynn, Wendy Craig, Brian Wilson of the Beach Boys, Lionel Richie.
JUNE 21st	Jane Russell, the equally large Alexander the Great, Prince William.

Cancer

Crabby Henry VIII

THE SIGN OF THE CRABBY.
JUNE 22nd – JULY 22nd

The first water sign – and therefore wet in every way.

Words often associated with Crabs – nasty rash, itching, clinic, pain when peeing.

Cancerians are frequently – possessive, self-pitying, tough on the outside but soft inside.

Famous Crabs – Ray Crabs, Donna Crabs, Sybil Fawlty, Meryl Streep, Henry VIII, Lady Di, Sylvester Stallone, Speverend Rooner.

Typical employer – Shell.

Greatest fear – John West.

Ruler – many say that their movements are ruled mainly by muesli, but more serious astrologers claim that the moods of the Crab are like those of the tide, totally in tune with the moon. This could explain why Cancerians get a rise every night and are unbelievably dim during the day.

WHAT THE EXPERTS SAY . . .

With your ruling ascendant combining celestial and physical influences, your chart is formulating an on-going long-range program situation with solar and stellar momentum at this moment in time, introducing elements which may or may not affect the movements of Uranus (i.e. they're talking out of their arses).

THE COMPLETE LIST OF CANCERIANS WHO ARE NOT POSSESSIVE . . .

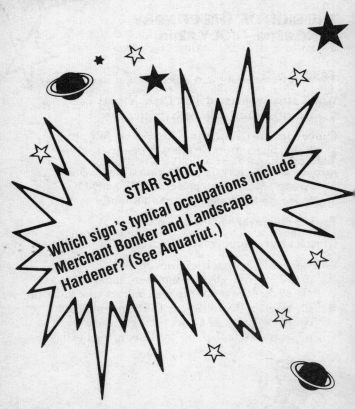

STAR SHOCK

Which sign's typical occupations include Merchant Bonker and Landscape Hardener? (See Aquariut.)

WHY DO THEY SOUND SO WET?

Just like their fellow Water signs, Pisceans, Cancerians's names frequently remind us of things that are wet . . . Virginia **Wade**, The Duke of **Well**ington, Alastair **Burn**et, Lor**rain**e Chase, Harrison **Ford**, Tim **Brook**e-Taylor, **Adam** Faith, Mick **Fleet**wood, Gina Lollo**bridg**ida, **Debb**ie Harry.

CANCER AND SEX

Like Cancerian Julius Caesar, it's all attack: 'I saw, I conquered, I came.' Cancerians still think foreplay is something that happens when two Geminis get together.

CANCERIANS CANNOT SURVIVE WITHOUT . . .

Water, money and food.

DOES YOUR CANCER MAN . . .

1. Makes passes at his mother? yes ☐ no ☐
2. Feel safer wearing a nappy? yes ☐ no ☐
3. Collect things he never uses but can never throw away? yes ☐ no ☐
4. Buy 'Girlie' magazines
   a) monthly? yes ☐ no ☐

   b) daily? yes ☐ no ☐

   c) hourly? yes ☐ no ☐
5. Hide under rocks on the beach? yes ☐ no ☐

DOES YOUR CANCER WOMAN . . .

1. Demand food after sex?
   Or during? Or instead of?   yes ☐ no ☐

2. Does she constantly diet,
   then get depressed, then
   revert to heavy drinking to
   compensate, then put on
   weight, then diet again?
   (No? Nor does mine.)   yes ☐ no ☐

3. Lust, ambition, drive? Has
   she any idea what these
   words mean?   yes ☐ no ☐

4. Does she still send off
   coupons for absolutely
   anything, so that people will
   think she receives post?   yes ☐ no ☐

5. Is she constantly afraid of
   catching Hypochondria?   yes ☐ no ☐

                                        maybe ☐

CANCER MAN

Misers. Moonies. Mummy's boys. Beneath that tough shell most crabs are wet inside. And true to their sign, they are always happiest when close to water. Look at Henry VIII with Hampton Court Palace on the Thames, or pop king Richard Branson who, despite his wealth, lived for years on a humble houseboat; or George Michael who surrounded himself with that drip Andrew Ridgeley, or John the Baptist or Ernest Hemingway who drank like a fish. This old man loves the sea all right, but he's just like a crab in many other ways too. For a start, when he's got his claws into something he wants, he'll never let go. Call it persistence, stubborness or pure bloody-mindedness, this is what gets successful Cancerians right to the top. Or the bottom, if they hold on like General Custer, whose famous last stand fell under Cancer. It's not at all unusual for these powerful creatures ruled by the Moon to be equally loony. Look at Henry VIII, who thought he had to employ an axe-man before his wives could give him head . . . Henry's also a great, not to say vast, example of the Cancerian love of food. He even shares a birthday with history's other fattest famous man, Cyril Smith, the MP who was only happy next to government 'wets'.

But Crabs can be just as jolly as they are fat. It's no coincidence that both *Punch* (or is it 'Paunch') magazine and its editor Alan Coren were both born under Cancer. Like Neil Simon and Tom Stoppard, the Crab can be as sharp a wit as he is a blunt boss. As for sticking his claws in just where it hurts, don't forget that the night of the long knives also happened under Cancer. In fact, the soldier Crab is a force to be reckoned with. Witness Sylvester Stallone. Maybe Rambo was one of the few who didn't get crabs in Vietnam, but he certainly got involved with 'crushed Asians' . . . Stallone, like Branson, George Michael, Ringo Starr, Pierre Cardin and Rembrandt, displays the typical Cancer capacity for amassing a fortune out of the Arts. And they attract a great deal of publicity too. It's no coincidence that one of Cancerian David Hockney's most famous painting is called 'A Bigger Splash'. Cancerians get splashed all over the media! The women even more so. Nancy Reagan and Lady Di are just two famous Crabs who love being surrounded by drips.

CANCER WOMAN

Just like their ruler the Moon, Cancerian women can be incredibly round (Barbara Cartland), empty (Lady Di), high every night (Debbie Harry), rarely visited by men (Emily Pankhurst), ghostly white (Nancy Reagan), surrounded by stars (Meryl Streep), regularly on the wax (Linda Ronstadt), or the wane (Virginia Wade), with a dark side (Mary Magdalene), and a blue (University Boat race cox, Sue Brown). Only occasionally do they appear to beam, but that's only because, like Cancerian Esther Rantzen, they have huge teeth.

Ms Rantzen is typically Cancerian in that, once she's got her claws into someone, she'll never let go.

As is the woman we've seen as the crabbiest creature on Earth, Prunella Scales, whose Sybil Fawlty was the perfect Cancer. Always fussing, insisting that she managed the money and that no one else ever had a say. The Cancerian woman's need to be associated with things watery includes not only Nancy Reagan and Lady Di's desire to marry drips, but also their passion for harbouring things – grudges, complaints, regrets, disappointments – which is why people ruled by the Moon are so regularly blue. They are incurable romantics of the soppiest sort, dreaming of the Mills and Boon world of Cancerian novelist Barbara Cartland, where the stories are even more made up than she is. Someone like Lady Di, totally divorced from the world, is a perfect example of the Cancerian woman as frowner and frenetic dieter. As is Lorraine Chase or Virginia Wade. When was the last time you saw her looking less highly strung than her racquets?

The only time that Cancerian women stop worrying about things is when they lose themselves in their music . . . like Lady Di with her permanently attached Walkma'am . . . and they'll listen to anything soppy. The favourite song for the Crab that loves to feel protected? 'Mee-shell.'

Cancerian women are as over-protective as they are over-possessive, which is why they make all their sons such softies. The most macho son of Cancer being Wayne Sleep.

Sex and the Cancerian girl? Well, the first cat show ever held was genuinely held during Cancer. There were plenty of pussies on display but the claws came out if anyone was stupid enough to touch.

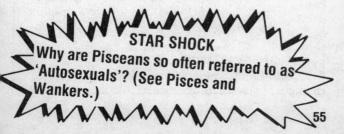

STAR SHOCK
Why are Pisceans so often referred to as 'Autosexuals'? (See Pisces and Wankers.)

THE NIPPERS

Cancerian children display the Crab's characteristic love of hoarding, being those annoying brats who've always got a sweet left long after everyone else has finished. And of course, crab children believe in Santa Claws.

PRINCE CHARLES CONTROLLED FROM OUTER SPACE!

Future King's Ears Manoeuvred by Martians! Lost City of Atlantis Found in Los Angeles Pool! Secret of Eternal Youth Not Discovered in Gay Goldfish! I Was a Teenage Window-box!

These are just some of the startling revelations made by ordinary people after subscribing to the legendary Terry the Tarot fortune-telling classes in Llandudno Voodoo Centre.

And you too can see the inner life by sending £50 a week to Terry the Tarot. Existing disciples have already made contact with extra-terrestrials, learnt the wonders of crystal gazing and made some potent home brews.

SEND NOW to Terry the Tarot, 34 Pillock Street, Llandudno, gateway to Pontypridd.

CANCER MAN – ARIES WOMAN

Take a Cancer man like Sylvester Stallone, there's certainly plenty of Ram in Rambo, but there's also BO, especially with the heartier variety of Cancer and, unlike Sagittarian women, who form the greater part of the great unwashed, Aries girls are moderately hygienic. They get hot certainly, but they like their sweat fresh. If Aries woman comes across the unhearty kind of Cancer, her fire sign passion will soon be put out by his wetness, however much she asks him to get ardour . . . Beware, many Cancer men love practical jokes that will make you laugh; like taking their pyjamas off.

CANCER MAN – TAURUS WOMAN

You've only got to look at Taurean women like Ella Fitzgerald or Victoria Wood to know that they love eating just as much as Crabs. And Cancer man loves playing host to hungry guests; he's usually quite a good cook. The problem with mixing an Earth sign with a Water sign is that things get pretty muddy . . . and basic Bulls are going to find murky Cancerians like Ken Russell far too dirty. She'll be hoping he'll wine and dine her before saying, 'Did the Earth sign move for you?' He's more likely to ask if she gets turned on by nuns in suspenders . . .

CANCER MAN – GEMINI WOMAN

They could make history together. A Gemini woman of the Joan Collins variety could give Cancerian Henry VIII more head than all six wives put together. But he'll hate her if she teases him or tries to creep out from under his shell. Cancer man likes to reign supreme with all his underlings fixed firmly in place. No place for restless Gemini. These independent career women rarely settle down to have nippers.

CANCER MAN – CANCER WOMAN

They hate each other's constant clawing. A disastrous relationship.

★ CANCER WOMAN – CANCER MAN

A fantastic relationship. Especially if confined to business partnership, friendship, sexual affairs, romance, camaraderie or marriage. The only problem being how to decide which shell to move into.

☆ CANCER MAN – LEO WOMAN ☆★

As the man who loves to pamper and support, he'll make her a wonderful doormat. The rich Cancerians include not only Buddy Rich, Rich Branson and John D. Rockefeller, but also Pierre Cardin. Between them they've got everything it takes to entertain a Lioness like the rich man's Liz Taylor – Princess Margaret. If anyone can drink and drain a Water sign dry, it's a Leo. Even a Cancerian as powerful as Julius Caesar would find a Leo, like Cleo, bound to roam.

☆☆ CANCER MAN – VIRGO WOMAN

What's a wealthy Crab like Richard Branson likely to do with a Virgin? Use her to attract more toyboy musicians to his empire? The trouble with Virgo women is that, like Agatha Christie, they love to pry, love to start having a hand in the running of things, and Cancer men like their hidden depths to stay hidden. But Virgo women adore manipulating rich men. Take Sue Ellen (Linda Gray); look at the number of Oil Barons' balls she's handled . . .

☆☆ ★ CANCER MAN – LIBRA WOMAN

If he's one of the really tough Cancer guys like Sylvester Stallone, he could get on extremely well with a determined Libra like Maggie Thatcher; they're equally diplomatic. But Crabs like to hide under things Rocky because they're usually soft inside. Libra women get tougher the deeper you go. Look how Maggie's got supposedly tough-guy Cancerian Richard Branson to start picking up all her litter . . .

CANCER MAN – SCORPIO WOMAN

Provided this lover of status symbols can stop farting in the bath to try and convince her he's got a jacuzzi, this could be a great relationship, many say it produces exceptional children. Well, anything with ten pairs of pincers and a claw-like tail has got to be classed as an extraordinary nipper.

CANCER MAN – SAGITTARIUS WOMAN

An unusually explorative Cancer like Sir Edmund Hillary could literally get on top of a mountainous Sagittarienne like Bette Midler. One look at those twin peaks and he'd be busy preparing first base down below. But though having a secure base might appeal to Crabs, it's the last thing a Sagbag is interested in. She's only concerned with being base. And he'll be heartbroken at the typical Sagittarian trait of describing all her previous lovers in lurid detail. What if she had Crabs before she met him?

CANCER MAN – CAPRICORN WOMAN

(They've just had a row and they're still not speaking, so it's hard to say more than that!)

CANCER MAN – CAPRICORN MAN

The problems high-climbing Capricorns have understanding the often unbelievably cretinous Crabs all started out when Cancerian John the Baptist showed his delight at meeting Capricorn Jesus by dunking Him in a river. Further theological problems continued with Cancerian the Reverend Spooner . . . nobody took kindly to hearing that Our Lord was born in the 'dome of a honkey', or that He gave us our 'braily dead' and finally 'cried on the doss' . . .

CANCER MAN – AQUARIUS WOMAN

They could get on extremely well provided they never discussed her 'interests'. Like all Wet Borers, Aquarian woman soon becomes a self-appointed expert on anything and everything from whether placenta omelettes make babies more immune to whether men see Laura Ashley wallpaper as a threat to their superiority. Remember Aquarius woman is the Burn-Your-Bras-To-Stop-Them-Nuking-Gay-Seals Brigade . . . Germaine Queer, Virginia Woooooolf, Vanessa Red-and-incredibly-grave. It is a well-known fact that the world's first shrink got the idea from a date with an Aquarian woman.

CANCER MAN – PISCES WOMAN

Let's face it, a Pisces is bloody grateful to get any partner. Though a Fish settling down with a Crab is hardly adventurous – it's the first sign to come along. And no doubt Cancer man will view Pisces woman as the ghoul next door . . . sexually speaking, her typical Pisces fantasies can get very strange indeed . . . a Minnoes-à-trois? a midnight dip with forty Fins? Even a beach boy like Cancer will be surprised at what goes on on the sea bed.

FUTURE FORECAST

In the coming year, Cancerians will continue to walk sideways and pinch things . . .

STAR SHOCK

Geminis are very good at pretending to be somebody important. See Mike Yarwood or Prince Philip.

SAGITTARIUS SHOCK

Botham rubs his balls in public! See Sagittarian Man to discover just why they all have penis envy.

61

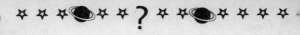

ARE YOU AS CRABBY

BORN:

JUNE 22nd Prunella Scales, Esther Rantzen, Meryl Streep, Kris Kristofferson, Cyndi Lauper.

JUNE 23rd Adam Faith.

JUNE 24th John the Baptist, Mick Fleetwood, Claud Chabrol.

JUNE 25th Custer's Last Stand, George Michael (Andrew Ridgeley's last stand), Eddie Large, Carly Simon.

JUNE 26th Willy Messerschmitt, Laurie Lee.

JUNE 27th Alan Coren, Helen Keller, Tommy Cannon.

JUNE 28th Henry VIII and the considerably larger Cyril Smith, John Inman.

JUNE 29th Oxbridge cox Sue Brown.

JUNE 30th Buddy Rich. The night of the long knives.

JULY 1st Lady Di, Debbie Harry, Olivia de Havilland.

JULY 2nd David Owen, the Duke of Wellington.

JULY 3rd Ken Russell, Tom Stoppard, Franz Kafka.

JULY 4th Neil Simon, Louis Armstrong, Gina Lollobrigida.

JULY 5th Elizabeth Emanuel, Mark Cox.

JULY 6th Nancy Reagan, Sylvester Stallone, Dave Allen.

JULY 7th Ringo Starr, Pierre Cardin, Marc Chagall, Gustav Mahler.

AS THIS LOT?

JULY 8th	John D. Rockefeller, Ferdinand von Zeppelin.
JULY 9th	Barbara Cartland, David Hockney, Ted Heath.
JULY 10th	Virginia Wade, Arthur Ashe.
JULY 11th	Yul Brynner.
JULY 12th	Julius Caesar, Alastair Burnet, Chris Quinten, 'Brian' from *Coronation Street*.
JULY 13th	Harrison Ford.
JULY 14th	Gerald Ford, Ingmar Bergman, Emily Pankhurst.
JULY 15th	Linda Ronstadt, Hammond Innes, Rembrandt, Cliff Barnes.
JULY 16th	Lorraine Chase, Ginger Rogers, Stewart Copeland.
JULY 17th	James Cagney, Tim Brooke-Taylor, Wayne Sleep, Donald Sutherland.
JULY 18th	Richard Branson, John Glenn, William Makepeace Thackeray.
JULY 19th	Ilie Nastase, the first Men's Wimbledon Final – 1877.
JULY 20th	Diana Rigg, Sir Edmund Hillary.
JULY 21st	Ernest Hemingway, Jonathan Miller, Cat Stevens.
JULY 22nd	Reverend Spooner lorn in Bondon, Himmy Jill, Mary Magdalene.

Leo

THE SIGN OF PRIDE AND PREJUDICE
JULY 23rd–AUGUST 23rd

Leos love – everything beginning with 'fl' . . . flattery, flirting, flaunting, flamboyance, flanelling, flings, flashiness, flatulence, flowers for the women, fleshpots, floozies and f-latio for the men . . . but their fondness for letting wine flow by the flagon always turns Leos to flab, (the thing Leo Terry Wogan is always fighting).

Famous Lions – Lenny the Lion, Elsa, Mick Jagger, Jackie Onassis, Napoleon, Princess Margaret, Benito Mussolini, Danny La Rue, Mata Hari, Madonna, Alexei Sayle.

Fave film – *Born Free*, the philosophy they keep for life.

To understand the Lion, just listen to the songs from the leader of the pack . . .

'GET OFF MY CLOUD'

The King of the Jungle always has a huge sense of his own importance. Eight out of ten owners say their big cats have to be petted, patted and pampered with no expense spared. This is the sign of the ego-maniac, the snob, the top cat, the creature who's only happy when he's high up above everybody else. Leos have got to have the Lion's share of everything; with everybody else subservient . . .

SCORPIO SHOCK
Why do so few people fancy a sting in their tail? (See Scorpio – Rock Hudson's rising sign.)

'UNDER MY THUMB'

This is the sign of the dictator all right . . . Napoleon, Mussolini, Fidel Castro, George Bernard Shaw. Leo is a Fire sign with a Fixed astrological quality. And it's true, once they get heated, there's no shifting them. You've just got to grant them their pleasure . . .

'SATISFACTION'

There's nothing a Leo loves more than being in the limelight, ruling the world of entertainment, like Leos Mick Jagger, Robert Redford, Dustin Hoffman, Sean Penn and Madonna. Charismatic on stage with their Fire sign burning bright, but once the spotlight is off them, they can be hot-tempered and flaming unbearable. Every Leo needs an audience, and the bigger the better. Look at Leo Cecil B. de Mille. This extravagant beast didn't care if a cast of thousands meant a cost of thousands. They adore the massive spectacular. Which is probably why the first Olympic games were held during Leo, or why Leo Olympic champion Daley Thompson rises to the challenge of not just one event, but ten. Leos always want more. Of everything. They're like opera singers . . . loud, full of extravagant gestures, adoring lavish costumes, making grand entrances, and having melodramatic moods, taking over ritzy restaurants after the evening's first performance to give yet another. And Leo's vast appetite extends far beyond food . . .

'LET'S SPEND THE NIGHT TOGETHER'

There's nowhere that Leos love to indulge themselves more than in the bedroom. Forget comparative wimps like Casanova; French Leo Alexandre Dumas is genuinely supposed to have fathered over five hundred children. God only knows how he found the time to do all that writing.

And Leo women? Well, do you honestly believe that tousled temptress Madonna is really anything 'like a virgin'? What about the theatre critic's crumpet, Helen Mirren? Or Princess Margaret? She's had plenty of rakes in her back garden. As for Mick Jagger, only a Leo could bring out an LP showing an unzippable pair of flies and called 'Sticky Fingers' . . . and we all know how cocky he used to be about his 'Little Red Rooster' . . . but they just can't be tamed . . .

'THE MIDNIGHT RAMBLER'

The call of the wild will always attract a Leo. And it's incredible how much they can get around. Look at Alan Whicker or Susan George or Neil Armstrong, who took his first small step on August 5th, under Leo. Take the Leo Emperor Claudius, who was always bound to roam . . . you just can't keep a Lion caged. Especially at night . . . remember Dustin Hoffman in *Midnight Cowboy*? Or Terry Wogan? Every bloody night he just rambles on and on . . .

'HONKY TONK WOMEN'

And where do they ramble to? Well, Lions are just like those other big cats, cheetahs, in every respect . . . there's nothing that gets a Leo man more turned on than sexy underwear, silks and stockings. And they love it when women wear them too. Don't imagine that a Lioness like Jackie Onassis caught her man by talking about business; that was all Greek to her. And you don't really think Madonna wears support tights and thermal underwear? Leos have other ways of keeping bodies hot. And it's not just the women that love playing the vamp: that Queen of the Jungle, drag artist Danny la Rue, has often been called 'Honky Tonk' . . . every Lion loves being wicked . . .

'SYMPATHY FOR THE DEVIL'

The King of the Beasts can be evil as hell. Look at Mata Hari, the seductive double agent. Never trust a Lioness not to kiss and tell *and* exaggerate along the way. And they're not just the stars of skinflicks . . . those evil movies *The Shining* and *A Clockwork Orange* were both directed by a Leo, Stanley Kubrick. Just like the Rolling Stones, every Leo has a way of stirring Hell's Angels . . .

'PAINT IT BLACK'

All those dark mysteries penned by P. D. James are written by a Leo. So too is the black humour of Dorothy Parker and Richard Ingrams of *Private Eye*. And the world's most famous private eye, Philip Marlowe was created by a Leo Raymond Chandler. They adore the intrigue of the criminal mind and the evil in women . . . 'She was a blonde to make a bishop kick a hole in a stained-glass window,' wrote Chandler. She was probably a Leo too.

The Lion is frequently associated with a darker nature . . . like Leo newsreader Trevor MacDonald, or *Pot Black* snooker star, Steve 'I-am-interesting-really' Davis, or car manufacturer, Henry Ford, who'd build you a car in 'Any colour, so long as it's black.' But if anyone else starts painting a Leo as black, they start to roar. In fact, even the slightest criticism will make them cry . . .

'AS TEARS GO BY'

Every Leo turns to tears sooner or later. Like Leo Gene Kelly, they're always 'singing in the reign', but if anyone takes their place at the top, they're distraught. Impulsive to the end, they will never debate a point gently, simply turn and roar – then get roaring drunk when rebuffed. Remember how upset Napoleon was when Josephine said, 'Not tonight, darling, I've got another frog in my throat'?

And Leos can never say sorry. As for admitting 'It's my fault', the pride of lions would never allow it. Which is why their lives can be littered with so many mistakes and upsets . . .

'19TH NERVOUS BREAKDOWN'

When Shakespeare said that that ancient temptress Cleopatra 'Had died twenty times', it was because the Leo in Cleo had already had nineteen nervous breakdowns. They can never get enough off their chests (like Leo Mae West). The Lion will always regret something . . . the way their generous gestures always lead to budgetary disasters, leaving them like Leo Mark Knopfler, in dire straits . . . or the way they leap into *Love At First Bite*, like George Hamilton. Leos are always too hasty, like that Lion in winter, Napoleon, rushing to invade Russia before reading the weather forecast . . . that's just the sort of mammoth operation the Lion will charge into without thinking. Which is why, like Lioness Barbara Windsor or that other Windsor, Princess Margaret, Leos always make huge tits of themselves.

Roaring . . . rolling . . . stoned . . . it's hard to believe Leos were ever in the cubs.

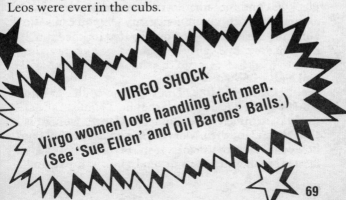

VIRGO SHOCK

Virgo women love handling rich men. (See 'Sue Ellen' and Oil Barons' Balls.)

69

☆ LEO MAN – ARIES WOMAN

Fiery Aries just isn't going to be dictated to by a Leo like Mussolini. She won't take all that lip from Jagger either, but that's what she'll get, because, whilst other signs may allow the first zodiac sign to be put first in everything, Leo will never give up his limelight. And the flash Lion is bound to be overshadowed by a big Aries like Samantha Fox. Up against her, his chest medallions would never see the light of day.

✸ LEO MAN – TAURUS WOMAN

The Bianca–Mick Jagger relationship. What went wrong? Simple, timid Taureans will never be Lion-tamers. What's a shy little Bull supposed to say to a lascivious Leo like Napoleon? 'Not tonight darling, I don't want a frog in my throat'? That other French Leo, Alexandre Dumas, is genuinely supposed to have spawned over five hundred baby frogs . . . No, there's only one Leo who revels in a load of bull – Terry Wogan.

★ LEO MAN – GEMINI WOMAN

A starred romance for the Air triplicity and mutable quadruplicity, Gemini, like their ruler Mercury (messenger of the gods and liquid we put in thermometers), with duality accented if planetary placings combine substantial Sun and Moon ascendants with Venus versatility. As you can see, Gemini girls are just too complicated for the Lion. He likes an easy lay.

☆ LEO MAN – CANCER WOMAN

Well, a Cancerian like Nancy Reagan could get into trouble alongside a Leo. All that heat could make all that plastic melt . . . Leo man and Cancer woman is the Dustin Hoffman/Meryl Streep relationship. Look how well *Kramer v. Kramer* got on together. It's also Benito Mussolini versus Emmeline Pankhurst, and

70

let's face it, the typically ultra-chauvinistic Leo still thinks a suffragette is someone who lives near Heathrow. And give a Leo like Alfred Hitchcock a crabby woman and you might as well drop the 'H' from his name!

LEO MAN – LEO WOMAN

Napoleon and Princess Margaret, Madonna and Sean Penn. Both will always want to be pampered and pawed more than the other, both will want to be king of the animals. This is a disastrous pairing. Unless they get on really well together, the pride of Lions will never allow anyone else to feel superior. Dividing the Lion's share will hurt even more. In their pathetic attempts to be pitied and seduced at the same time, both Leos will wimper, 'Poor me, paw me . . .'

LEO MAN – VIRGO WOMAN

How could the pride of Lions ever give in to the bossy Elizabeth I type of woman? He's not going to let her trample over his raincoat to avoid puddles, that would stain the Pierre Cardin logo and embroidered initials. No, flash man will never get on with over-hygienic Virgo. She'll hate him doing only what his lazy self considers the absolute minimum to get by. Haven't you noticed how Leo men only iron their collars and cuffs? They know their suit will cover up most of their shirt.

LEO MAN – LIBRA WOMAN

Would Mussolini and Napoleon stand a chance with Thatcher? Of course not. A Libran woman like that could show him just what a nation of greengrocers and corner-shop-owners can become. And Librans just aren't showy like Leos. They like to work behind the scenes, pull the strings and give anyone their final curtain.

71

★ LEO MAN – SCORPIO WOMAN

A hot-bed of passion barely describes what Mick the lips and Loretta 'Hotlips' Swit could get up to, but once the fling is flung, cunning Scorpio will always beat flash Leo at his own game. Remember, Leos are the men who try to impress you at traffic lights by talking into expensive car-phones they cannot afford. Scorpios are just as impressive on the car-phone, but infinitely more economical, since they never have the car-phone actually connected to anything, well aware that other motorists can't see below window level.

✪ LEO MAN – SAGITTARIUS WOMAN

Mick Jagger and Tina Turner? They're just as dirty as each other on-stage, but off-stage Sagittarian women have personal habits that are even too dubious for lazy, all-show Leos. A dynamic fire sign like Leo she may be, but can you really put up with her spraying perfume on her clothes rather than washing them? And Sagbags are far too lazy to pamper the jungle king, and that's what Leos need. Remember, this is the man who complained to his doctor that his wife was so ill he had to carry her downstairs to get him his drink.

★ LEO MAN – SAGITTARIUS MAN

A Leo like Danny la Rue probably loves riding horses . . . and they can be great sports, Sagittarian boys . . . But someone like Centaur Ian Botham will have far more in common with a Leo like Neil Armstrong: both make the headlines when they're spaced out.

✡ LEO MAN – CAPRICORN WOMAN

Mick Jagger and Marianne Faithful; both ruled by Mars, and that's not the planet . . . (it's best not to dwell on what inspired him to write 'Brown Sugar').

If you're the type of Leo who's got a mountain of money, Capricorn girls like Princess Michael will climb right up on the top . . . it's amazing what they can get up to when other people are paying.

LEO MAN – CAPRICORN WOMAN

Two of a kind. Capricorn women include Ava
Gardner, something Leo Princess Margaret loved to
do . . .

LEO MAN – AQUARIUS WOMAN

Maybe Mussolini would have got on or even off with
Natasha Kinski – both had a little Roman in them . . .
but Leos like the centre of every conversation to be
themselves, they'll hate the Water-bearer bearing
down on them with their endless outpourings and
theories. The only Leo who would put up with them
is Steve 'I-am-interesting-really' Davis, hoping to pick
up some interesting pieces of information to use in
conversation, should that ever occur . . .

LEO MAN – PISCES WOMAN

All cats hate getting wet and, let's face it, nobody gets
wetter than Pisces. The Catfish relationship is
therefore very unlikely. Whereas Leos can be
melodramatic, it's usually all put on for effect; Pisces
get weepy because they're generally having a real
crisis (this regularly happens after looking in the
mirror). Over a typical Leo/Pisces dinner, Leo man
would be roaring drunk; Pisces woman would sip a
moderate amount of carrot juice. He would tear into
the red meat; she would order lentils and then say a
poem to the Vegetable Gods explaining the heavy
concept of uprooting one of their fellow spirits.

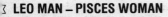

IN THE COMING YEAR . . .

All Leo drivers will continue to promote the
lay in lay-by . . .

73

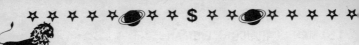

ARE YOU AS WILD

BORN:

JULY 23rd	David Essex, Michael Foot, Coral Browne, Raymond Chandler.
JULY 24th	Robert Graves, Alexandre Dumas.
JULY 25th	Lynne Frederick and the first test tube baby.
JULY 26th	Mick Jagger, Susan George, Vitas Gerulaitis, Stanley Kubrick, Helen Mirren, Danny La Rue, Carl Jung, George Bernard Shaw, Aldous Huxley.
JULY 27th	Shirley Williams, Jo Durie, Hilaire Bollock.
JULY 28th	Jackie Onassis, Beatrix Potter.
JULY 29th	Benito Mussolini.
JULY 30th	Daley Thomson, Clive Sinclair, Kate Bush, Henry Ford, Emily Brontë.
JULY 31st	Geraldine Chaplin.
AUGUST 1st	Claudius, Yves St Laurent.
AUGUST 2nd	Alan Whicker, Len Murray.
AUGUST 3rd	Terry Wogan, Rupert Brooke, P. D. James. (Murder, mystery and suspense . . .)
AUGUST 4th	Percy Bysshe Shelley.
AUGUST 5th	Neil Armstrong took his first small step on Earth.
AUGUST 6th	Robert Mitchum, Frank Finlay, Barbara

AS THESE LIONS?

	Windsor, Lucille Ball, Lord Alfred Tennyson.
AUGUST 7th	Mata Hari.
AUGUST 8th	Dustin Hoffman, Andy Warhol.
AUGUST 9th	Rod Laver, John Dryden, Whitney Houston.
AUGUST 10th	Kate O'Mara, Eddie Fisher.
AUGUST 11th	Sir Angus Wilson.
AUGUST 12th	Mark Knopfler, Fulton MacKay, Cecil B. de Mille, George Hamilton.
AUGUST 13th	Fidel Castro, William Caxton, Fergal Sharkey.
AUGUST 14th	John Galsworthy.
AUGUST 15th	Princess Anne, Napoleon, Lawrence of Arabia.
AUGUST 16th	Madonna, Trevor MacDonald, Ted Hughes. Elvis Presley died.
AUGUST 17th	Sean Penn, Mae West, Robin Cousins, Robert de Niro, Davy Crockett.
AUGUST 18th	Robert Redford, Casper Weinberger.
AUGUST 19th	Richard Ingrams, Ogden Nash.
AUGUST 20th	The author's mother – and look what she gave birth to . . .
AUGUST 21st	Princess Margaret, Barry Norman.
AUGUST 22nd	Steve Davis, Dorothy Parker.
AUGUST 23rd	Geoff Capes, Gene Kelly, Willy Russell.

Virgo

✱ ✱ £ ✱ ✱ $ ✱ ✱ 🪐 ✱ ✱ $ ✱ ✱ £ ✱ ✱

THOSE VIRGIN ON THE OBSCENE
AUGUST 24th – SEPTEMBER 23rd

Don't believe them – forget everything the name Virgo suggests . . . Raquel Welch is a Virgo (apparently Britt Ekland never was . . .)

On the surface	Underneath
They appear hygienic	This is just a cover for their natural dirtiness.
They say they need lots of sleep	Yes, they're often in bed by 8.30 . . . but never home before 12.00.
They say they're just horsing around	Don't forget Caligula was a Virgo . . . .
They say they're untouched by human hand	It's true . . . the hands were well into the plural.

People who claim they're still Virgos – Raquel Welch, Sophia Loren, Linda Gray ('Sue Ellen'), Larry Hagman ('J.R.'), D. H. Lawrence, the girl in the film *Animal House* who insisted on wearing surgical gloves when handling her boyfriend.

Typical Job – sex goddess, author of filthy books, mother of Messiah, person who writes 'pure' on fruit juice cartons, the inventor of the in-flight sick-bag and the domestic pets' 'pooper-scooper', blackhead remover in beauticians.

Fave hobbies – glueing people's knees together, giving vasectomies, sniffing milk, ironing underwear.

Fave group – Hymen Corner.

Fave Virgo vegetables – cucumbers, marrows, Mark Phillips (anything that resembles a prick).

ROYAL SHOCK

On March 10th, the birthday of London's Bakerloo line, which Prince started royalty going down the tube? (See Edward under Pisces Wimps.)

Origins – the name Virgo comes from the Latin phrase 'Cogito Virgo Sum', which means 'I'm still thinking about it, therefore I'm still a virgin. Needless to say, when most Virgos are asked, 'Are you a virgin?', they generally reply, 'Not yet.'

Astro-jargon – being the sixth sign of the zodiac, Virgo is an Earth element with a mutable quality, which roughly translated means, they can be real sods and often look like mutants.

Virgo with the sun in ascendency – relatively large numbers of Virgos share Sun characteristics, i.e. the ones in England are never very bright, the Mediterraneans are permanently on heat and many are covered in spots.

THE THINGS VIRGOS NAG ABOUT

(Being published separately. In fact this will be the only book with more entries than the *Encyclopaedia Brittanica*.)

HEALTH AND HYPOCHONDRIA

As health-freaks and eternal pessimists, Virgos always put prunes on their muesli.

VIRGOS LOVE . . .

Bulk containers of athlete's foot powder, picking other people's hairs out of the family soap, artificial insemination (though some of the bigger men find it hard fitting into the test tube).

VIRGO AND SEX

(That's not to say that they don't have it, just that they're not seen to have it. After all, this is the sign of the schemer . . .)

VIRGO MAN ★★☆★★

The biggest schemer under the Sun. This is the sign of
'J.R.'. Precise but never hygienic. This type of man
can be as dirty as he likes and continue to clean up in
every business venture. Beneath their neat exteriors,
these methodical men are often coldly calculating,
plotting something evil with their characteristic eye
for nastiness. Look at thriller writer Frederick Forsyth
or Roald Dahl or John Buchan, who took his first
famous steps under Virgo. The women are even bigger
plotters . . . Elizabeth I, Agatha Christie and the
creator of *Frankenstein*, Mary Shelley; she gave birth
to the best-looking Virgo around. The others tend to
look a bit freakish . . . Elliot Ghould, macho-man
Derek Nimmo, Michael 'Am-I-a-boy-or-a-girl'
Jackson, Denis Healy . . . note how most Virgo men
only have one eyebrow . . . in fact politics is not a
good profession for a Virgo, they've far too much
nervous energy – look how George Brown got his
knickers in a twist, or how Cecil Parkinson got
everyone else's, giving rise to whole new meanings
for parliamentary 'positions' . . .

The fact that California was born a Virgo (created
on September 9th), just shows what a weird sexual
state this sign can become – the emperor Caligula
being the worst case reported so far. So watch out if
your Virgo man says he's feeling a little hoarse; when
Caligula said he felt like an Italian stallion in bed, he
meant it literally . . . and he had nothing on that
Virgoan American gigolo, Richard Gere.

In public, Virgo man will dress ridiculously neatly,
with razor-sharp creases, precisely tied ties and super-
clean shoes. And Virgo men are always clean-shaven
– unless they have beards. But beneath that clean
exterior, they're as Earthy as Virgo D. H. Lawrence.
Mention chas-tity and they'll be thinking of Lady Di
. . . These Earth signs are tight-fisted sods too . . .
wasn't it a Virgo who wanted to know when Band Aid
were having a sale? But even though they can be

quick off the mark, like Virgos James Hunt and Stirling Moss, Virgo man is not necessarily a quick thinker . . . look at Mark Phillips, still re-taking his Eleven-plus.

Virgo man may smile with brilliantly clean teeth, like Barry Gibb, famous for his 'Mass o' chew sets', but they never have a completely clean record. Virgo man loves evil schemes, like 'J.R.', loves dirty jokes, like Russ Abbott and Lenny Henry; adores uncovering your secrets in bed, like Sean Connery; and likes getting his tongue round 'leedle girls', like Maurice Chevalier. Virgo philosopher Confucius say when Virgo man like William Golding say he want show you his *Lord of the Flies*, he no mean the book . . .

SPORTS SHOCK

Why is April 9th a great day for swingers? (Look under Aries.)

VIRGO WOMAN

It is no coincidence that the world's first carpet sweeper was born on September 19th, a Virgo. On first impression, every Virgoan is spotless. You never see them with unwashed hair or less than immaculate dress. Of course, this is all just a front. Look at 'Sue Ellen' with all that trashy Valentine lingerie. Underneath, like all Earth signs, these dirty sods have been well soiled. The fussy, neat exterior is just a cover. Though Virgo women are always hard to please. Just like Virgo sex goddesses Raquel Welch, Sophia Loren and Jacqueline Bisset and, of course, the Virgin Mary, when it comes to sex, only a god will do. Fortunately for us mere mortals, Virgo women include not only the exceptionally fastidious, but some exceptionally fast idiots.

In every case, Virgo women survive on their nerves, and get on everybody else's. But they are masters at twisting people around their little fingers, like ace schemer Agatha Christie who, like many Virgo women showed that she could get through *Ten Little Indians* in just two nights. In positions of power they can manipulate men even more. Look at Queen Elizabeth I – outwardly the typical Virgo, prudish and easily shocked, unbending and critical; while in private she'd been knocking off even more courtiers than Spaniards. But, as with all Virgos, she was a master of disguise, as was Agatha Christie, and her mother too. At Agatha's birth the old man still had absolutely no idea whodunnit . . .

In sexual matters especially, Virgo women have to be on top. They hate being beaten – with canes just as much as at work. If there's any disciplining or teaching to be done, it has to be by the woman. Remember it was a Virgo, Anne Bancroft, who turned young Dustin Hoffman into *The Graduate*; Virgo 'Sue Ellen' who decided when that wimp 'Peder' was going to lose his virginity; the elder woman Jacqueline Bisset, who can still collect 'toyboys'.

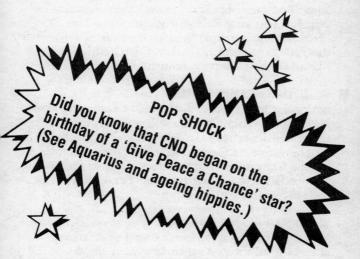

POP SHOCK

Did you know that CND began on the birthday of a 'Give Peace a Chance' star? (See Aquarius and ageing hippies.)

In fact the older Virgos get, the lustier they become. Just look at the author of *Lace*, Shirley Conran, combining the schemer's whodunnit plot with sexual fetishes like shoving goldfish down the heroine's knickers. But not all Virgos are weird. In fact, many are as outgoing and downright gregarious as Virgo Greta Garbo . . . the rest are more like Mary Shelley, creator of *Frankenstein*, a typical Virgo . . . the ghoul next door . . . Most Virgo girls agree with Virgo philosopher Confucius. He say, 'Virginity like a bubble; one prick, all gone.'

VIRGO MAN – ARIES WOMAN

A hot fire sign like Julie Christie will hate her Virgo man's coldly clinical habits, like wearing a sheath on each finger, or insisting on face masks whilst kissing. The only Virgo type that an Aries girl could be keen on is the more down-to-earth variety like Virgoan Confucius. He say, 'Man silly to give girlfriend piano, when he could give upright organ.'

★ VIRGO MAN – TAURUS WOMAN ★☆

Some Taureans can share Virgos love of neatness. Which is why cow-girls will admire Virgo Larry 'J.R.' Hagman. Though most Virgoan men can never keep their affairs in order . . . look at Cecil Parkinson . . . like all the best jokes, he brought down the house.

★ VIRGO MAN – GEMINI WOMAN ☆★★

Both ruled by Mercury, this could be a splendid affair. A kinky Virgo like Caligula will certainly appreciate the sexual appetite of Gemini 'Alexis Colby'. But the stricter variety of Gemini lady like Queen Victoria will be far from amused when a Virgoan of the Peter Sellers ilk keeps trying to impress her with what he calls his 'Pink Panther'.

☆ VIRGO MAN – CANCER WOMAN

Home-loving, loyal Cancerians will never trust quick-witted Virgo. As the name suggests, this is the sign that is always denying things. These are the men who come home late from the office party and insist that the stain on their trousers is toothpaste. Only a cretinous Crustacean like Lady Di would fall for an excuse like that.

★ VIRGO MAN – LEO WOMAN

The more wily variety of Virgo like 'J.R.' may well be able to manipulate a lusty Leo like Mata Hari or Princess Margaret or try to beat them at their own game. He'll call it spying, she'll say it's voyeurism but, this type excepted, most lusty Leos are far too impulsive to go along with a Virgoan's excessive caution, particularly the compulsory hoovering down of partners before foreplay.

VIRGO MAN – VIRGO WOMAN

The toughest match of all: The 'J.R.' v. 'Sue Ellen' relationship. Nobody will begin conversations with denials more than these two. Both are permanently trying to out-manipulate the other . . . both are bright, shrewd and critical . . . and both are very dirty under the clean public exterior. And Virgo women adore manipulating rich men; look at the way 'Sue Ellen' has handled all those Oil Barons' balls . . .

VIRGO MAN – LIBRA WOMAN

'J.R.' would surely meet his match with a Libran lady like Thatcher. So would Virgoan, Denis Thatcher. He'd loathe the Libran's liberal attitude towards spending. In fact, many Libran women still adhere to the belief that if it's for sale, one's duty-bound to buy. The Libra lady likes to think she can be perfectly ladylike of her own accord. She will therefore not take kindly to an over-hygienic Virgo sniffing not only his, but also her own armpits before dates.

VIRGO MAN – SCORPIO WOMAN

A cunning Virgo, full of neat endings (like Roald Dahl), is bound to appear to anyone who likes a sting in the tale, but other Scorpios may think Virgos are too honest. Remember, while Virgo drivers never take the polythene covers off their car seats, Scorpios are the sort of mechanics that put a polythene cover over your car seat and then charge you for a service. Sean Connery is a Virgo. James Bond was created a Scorpio; they're a shade more sly.

POP SHOCK Why are those born on May 8th connected with weird species?

85

★ VIRGO MAN – SAGITTARIUS WOMAN

Even a randy filly like Tina Turner will find a Virgo like Caligula's idea of horsing around a bit much. She'll hate his formality too; when God handed out tact, Sagittarians were in the wrong queue. The typically slothful Horse will never accept a Virgo's ridiculous demands for hygiene either. Remember, Virgos are the people who won't let firemen into a burning house unless they take their boots off first.

☆ VIRGO MAN – CAPRICORN WOMAN

Tight-fisted Virgo will certainly admire the even more miserly Capricorn, but a Capricorn like Diane Keaton will be far too capricious for orderly little Virgo. These are the men with unbelievably trim beards. They don't give their wives housekeeping money, they give ration-books. Far too bossy and critical for Capricorn. It would be just too easy for an old Goat like Joan of Arc to feel martyred, and Virgo man would never subscribe to the Capricorn's demands to be permanently referred to as 'Saint . . .'

☆ VIRGO MAN – PISCES WOMAN

The only Virgo man to which a fish dish is likely to appeal is the more earthy variety like D. H. Lawrence, the classic coupling being Virgo Sean Connery falling for Piscean Ursula Andress as she surfaced like Venus from the sea in the film *Doctor No*. However, more typical Virgo men will only have sex with a Pisces if they can keep their wet-suit and face-mask on.

IN THE COMING YEAR . . .

The few genuine Virgos that are still around will continue to believe that puberty is when men start beating around the bush and women start getting hold of the wrong end of the stick . . .

CONSULT THE CLAIRVOYANT THE PAPERS RECOGNIZE

'——— Clairvoyant ——— the
——— ———,' – The Times.

'A complete and utter dockhead.'
– The Grauniad.

'Mrs Rawalpindi is unbelievably
———,' The Standard.

'So real she could have been tape
recording what I told her . . .'
(Mug from Wapping).

Yes, everyone has something to say about Trace Rawalpindi's unique forecasts. 'More accurate than Michael Fish,' said one outpatient from a psychiatric ward. 'Your teachings have helped me survive without any of my previous wealth,' said one man on the £5000 a week course. 'What the fuck's going on?' said Analysed from Aldershot. Yes, it's a complete mystery how she does it, but GLASGOW's own psychic consultant and masseuse is waiting for you!

Send for free illustrated booklet to Trace Rawalpindi, 32 The Larches, Glasgow, Scotland.

ALSO PUBLISHED BY 'TRACE THE ACE'
* Reading the cards and lancing boils effortlessly.
* Hearing things in shells.
* Overcoming agrophobia and excessive ear wax.

BORN:

AUGUST 24th	Aubrey Beardsley, George Stubbs.
AUGUST 25th	Sean Connery, Frederick Forsyth, Leonard Bernstein, Elvis Costello.
AUGUST 26th	John Buchan, Christopher Isherwood.
AUGUST 27th	John Lloyd, Confucius, Sam Goldwyn.
AUGUST 28th	David Soul, Leo Tolstoy.
AUGUST 29th	Lenny Henry, James Hunt, Elliot Gould, Michael Jackson, Richard Gere.
AUGUST 30th	Denis Healey, John Peel, Mary Shelley, Muriel Gray.
AUGUST 31st	Larry Grayson, Caligula, James Coburn, Rocky Marciano, Richard Gere.
SEPTEMBER 1st	Cecil Parkinson (who does he think he's fooling), Barry Gibb.
SEPTEMBER 2nd	Jimmy Connors, George Brown.
SEPTEMBER 3rd	Raquel Welch, Nicky Horne.
SEPTEMBER 4th	Dinsdale Landen.
SEPTEMBER 5th	Russel Harty, Bob Newhart, Louis XIV, Jesse James, Freddie Mercury.
SEPTEMBER 6th	(Nobody born on this day is a Virgo any more.)
SEPTEMBER 7th	Elizabeth I, Anthony Quayle,

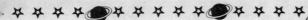

VIRGOS' ARE LYING?

	Malcolm Bradbury, Buddy Holly, Chrissie Hynde.
SEPTEMBER 8th	Michael Frayn, Jack Rosenthal, Harry Secombe, Siegfried Sassoon.
SEPTEMBER 9th	Cardinal Richelieu.
SEPTEMBER 10th	Judy Geeson, José Feliçiano.
SEPTEMBER 11th	D. H. Lawrence.
SEPTEMBER 12th	Linda 'Sue Ellen' Gray, Maurice Chevalier.
SEPTEMBER 13th	Jacqueline Bisset, Roald Dahl, Mel Tormé.
SEPTEMBER 14th	Angus Ogilvy.
SEPTEMBER 15th	Agatha Christie, Prince Harry, Jaki Graham.
SEPTEMBER 16th	Russ Abbott, Lauren Bacall.
SEPTEMBER 17th	Anne Bancroft, Stirling Moss.
SEPTEMBER 18th	Greta Garbo, (she didn't want anyone else added).
SEPTEMBER 19th	Twiggy, Zandra Rhodes, William Golding, Derek Nimmo.
SEPTEMBER 20th	Sophia Loren.
SEPTEMBER 21st	Larry 'J.R.' Hagman, Shirley Conran, Jimmy Young, H.G. Wells.
SEPTEMBER 22nd	Mark Phillips, commercial TV in Britain, in 1955.
SEPTEMBER 23rd	Bruce Springsteen, Ray Charles.

Libra

SIGN OF THE UNBALANCED
SEPTEMBER 24th – OCTOBER 23rd

Famous unbalanced Librans – Genghis Khan, Herod, Attila the Hun, Margaret Thatcher, and the stomach upset in *Alien*.

All Librans can be – very indecisive (unless there's the opportunity of sinking a *Belgrano* or letting another country store lethal weapons in yours).

Fave hobbies include – stabbing colleagues in the back, pretending that Britain is part of America, answering anything except questions.

Considerably more balanced Librans include – Richard III, Heinrich Himmler, King Kong.

Beautifully balanced Librans include – Brigitte Bardot, Sylvia Kristel, Catherine Deneuve.

The Libran who broke her scales – Sarah Ferguson.

But they are all – indecisive.

Typical Job – SDP mentor, Wimbledon linesman.

Fave colour – blue . . . or purple . . . maybe green . . . some reds are nice too . . .

Famous Libran quote – Please accept my resignation. I don't want to belong to any club that will accept me as a member. (Attributed to either Libran, Groucho Marx, or Libran, Maggie Thatcher on re-entering Parliament.)

Fave play – *Hamlet*.

THE BALANCE OF THE SEXES

In the case of a libidinous Libran like Sylvia Kristel, balance simply means having one person on each end. It is no coincidence that she was born on exactly the same day as Marks & Spencer's. Admittedly, 'Emmanuelle' is more into S & M than M & S, but they've both had a hand in thousands of people's underpants.

THE BALANCE OF POWER

A Libran like Maggie Thatcher loves balance, even if it requires police enforcement. She firmly believes that she is only being what all Librans want to be: honest. Libran politicians stab colleagues in the front.

THE BALANCED VIEW

All Librans hide behind the fact that people assume they are simply being indecisive. It's the perfect cover for radically changing their viewpoint from one extreme to the other. Take the Libran travelling by tube or on the bus: whilst they're waiting to squeeze on to the crowded vehicle, they take the view that everyone inside is a bastard for not making enough room; once they themselves have boarded, they think the people outside are idiots for thinking there's more room inside. The people who always feel a great sense of triumph when the tube doors shut on those waiting to get in are always Librans.

These are the people who become Labour politicians just as soon as they have got their own kids through public school, or the women who teach in comprehensive schools and drive home in their husbands' company Volvos. The Champagne Socialists of the Zodiac.

THE BALANCED DIET

Who put the **Bran** in **Li**bran? Eating muesli for Librans is not a health fad, simply a means of getting the evil they know they possess out of their system. Of course, it never works. The only result being that many Librans simply possess the ability to fly a kite when the weather's not windy.

THE BALANCE OF NATURE
Many Libran men become the wispy-bearded lefties that join Friends of the Earth and Brothers of the Gay Whale; shunning anything that is man-made. These are the ones who will only drink Real Ale and generally look like real aliens.

THE LIBRA DRIVER
Guaranteed to drive anyone sharing their roadspace round the bend. These are the indecisive nerds who indicate right before turning left. The people who tear off at the traffic lights in reverse. The people who park on 'Disabled' spaces because they assume that it includes the mentally incapable as well. Their favourite car? The Mini Metro Kamikaze. Many only use 'indicators' as a reminder of what they've just done. Still, they're better than Leos, who never indicate, assuming that everyone will be watching their showy limousines anyway. Leos think indicating is just for plebs.

BOOK SHOCK

Excluding Pisceans, what type of brain has most room at the top? (See April 13th or section on Thatcher under Libra.)

MOST ANNOYING HABITS

Never committing themselves; not to psychiatric wards, relationships, not even to the most trivial decisions. Ask a Libran if she'd like a drink . . . 'I'm all right,' she'll say. 'But what about your drink?' you reply. 'Well, are you having another?' she'll continue. 'I asked you first,' you respond. 'Well, if you're having one . . .' Librans will only drink a cup of tea, 'If you're putting the kettle on anyway.' Despite their characteristic love of shopping, any choices to be made will be heralded by that well-known Libran saying, 'Well, you decide.' These people say 'Eyther' one minute and 'Eether' the next. But, of course, once they get you to commit yourself to anything, Librans always point out that you made the wrong choice. (The only exception being when you vote Conservative.)

LIBRA MAN

Libra man can be like both types of Libra woman rolled into one: take Richard III . . . like libidinous Libran, Sylvia Kristel, he was one of history's biggest 'humpers', and like women's lib Libra, Maggie Thatcher, he was just a few goose-steps to the right of Attila the Hun. His funny hunched-up walk is a typical Libra trait . . . just look at Groucho Marx. With comments like, 'I never forget a face, but in your case I'll make an exception,' he too showed far more Libran diplomacy than Maggie Thatcher, but just the same level of Libran smarminess. In fact, Libran men make great SDP members – their favourite hobby is sitting on the fence. (Libran women simply stay put on defence . . .)

As a rule, Libran men always turn out to be less impressive than first impressions might suggest . . . take T. S. Eliot, who was in fact an anagram of 'Toilets' . . . or 'Superman' Christopher Reeve, once described as 'one hundred and eighty pounds of dynamite with a one-inch fuse' . . . or arch-poseur Bryan Ferry, often considered a bit of all right by the ladies (and one or two Libran men). But dear Bryan can never decide whether he should be playing the piano or adjusting his quiff. The fact that Libra is a cardinal sign means many of the men are thought to be 'Puffs'. What a mean thing to say about Cliff Richard! He displays the typical Libran trait of looking far younger than he really is, though like the other Young Ones, Libra man can be a complete bastard beneath that smoothie exterior . . . look at Leon Brittan . . . and talking of Librans that get laughed at, take Ronnie Barker – displaying the typical Libran need for harmony, he even likes to be balanced by another Ronnie. Another Libran joker was Buster Keaton, and nearly all Libran men are like him . . . best when they're silent. It's because they're all sinister under the surface, like Bob Geldof. They may start off as saints, but, like hit-man Roger Moore, it's never long before the saints are into bondage – and the evil ones not only include Evel Knievel, but the knieving Donald so-called Pleasanse, who played Bond's arch-enemy 'Blaufeldt' (exact counterpart to Libran Sylvia Kristel, also known as 'Blaujob').

An even more macabre Libran was Samuel Beckford, the Gothic novelist and at one time virtually the richest man in Britain. He lost his entire fortune through the typical Libran trait of not being able to say no . . . to gambling, lasciviousness, anything and everything. He finally died of that nasty social disease, Sagittarius. But then not all Librans make it rich . . . take Jimmy Carter, who was happy working for peanuts . . .

Overall, Libran men are never strong leaders, they are far too easily swayed, far too afraid of seeming unfair, far too hesitant to take advantage of everything that comes their way . . . they make great doormats for dominant women . . . they include far more Friends of the Earth than 'Real Men', in fact many Libran men can never fully decide which sex they are . . . Oscar Wilde, Gore Vidal, Nicholas Parsons . . . he only did *Sale of the Century* because he thought he'd meet 'salers' . . .

They may be effeminate, they may be about as exciting as limp lettuce, but every girl will find a Libran lover perfectly fair in bed. Unlike Sagittarians, who positively gallop out of their jockey shorts and reach their own finishing post just as quickly, girls should never forget that plodding Libra is the sign of Magnus Magnusson . . . 'I've started, so I'll finish . . .'

LIBRA WOMAN

The iron hand in the velvet glove. In Maggie's case, the iron hand in the nuclear glove. Libran women who work at it can nearly always get what they want. It's best not to think what Libra Linda McCartney did to catch Paul, but her going at it eight days a week provided her with the kind of balance Libran women love best, i.e. the one in the bank. Maggie Thatcher's hard work has paid off just as well. It was Libra man

Groucho Marx who said, 'I've worked myself up from nothing to a state of extreme poverty,' Maggie's worked herself up from nothing and in so doing, provided a state of extreme poverty. But that's Libra woman, always tipping the scales in her own favour. That's the positive type anyway, the women who put the **Lib** in **Lib**ra. The more negative Librans just stress the **bra**. Like women's libbers they're only too happy to have it off. Remember this is the sign of *Emmanuelle* star, Sylvia Kristel, the perfect example of the Libra woman who can't say no. All that stuff about Libran women thinking sex should be romantic? Forget it. If your Libra's not the type who uses her mind to get one over on people, then she's certainly the type who uses her body. Look at Bardot . . . when God created Libra woman, He must have been in Heaven weighing everything up! But of course the Libran sex goddess is not only outweighed by the dictator type – she's also balanced by her exact opposite, Julie Andrews. Whereas Sylvia Kristel would happily believe that Dick Van Dyke was three separate things, the Mary Poppins type Libran has only ever taken off with an umbrella. Putting the lib in 'libido' is not her idea of having a 'supercalifragilisticexpialidocious' time. No, the matron or governess Libra is very much more the upholder of strict Victorian values, like Thatcher. When it comes to sexual appetite, she's quite happy to starve . . . she certainly doesn't like 'crudités' for starters. Mary Poppins probably thinks fore-play is a super new type of hockey for family-size teams. The problem for most Libran women is simply deciding which type of woman they really are, or if they really are women at all . . . the problem with the career types being that they become more and more like men every day. In their desire for absolute balance between the sexes, they soon end up having, as Groucho Marx said, 'everything a man wants . . . a moustache, beard and muscles.' It is a well-known fact that the shadow cabinet is named after Maggie Thatcher's five o'clock beard.

One thing is certain, Libra women can get what they want without ever having to raise their voices. In fact, if they're like Linda McCartney, people prefer it if they don't. But it's true, Librans don't see the need to quarrel . . . like Thatcher, they just go on repeating their side of the argument so monotonously that most opponents finally give in, and whenever they are confronted with a suggestion they don't like, such as 'Don't you think it's time you stopped shopping?' or 'Wouldn't you prefer a son to a daughter?' or 'Don't you think nuking the neighbours is going a bit far?' – whenever they don't like what you're saying, Libran women bring into play their astonishing capacity for selective hearing. On the surface they therefore appear just as even-tempered as they are even-featured . . . of course, the real truth is that anyone thinking he's got this strange balancing act completely weighed up is soon to be outwitted . . . Libran women either are or possess bombshells – and like Thatcher or Olivia Neutron-Bomb, they rarely let a man put his finger on their button . . . (and would you really want to, anyway? Like Fergie, most Librans have scaly legs).

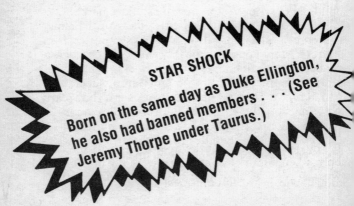

STAR SHOCK

Born on the same day as Duke Ellington, he also had banned members . . . (See Jeremy Thorpe under Taurus.)

LIBRA MAN – ARIES WOMAN

Everything you read about Arietians being great do-ers isn't true. Many of the women are like Aries Samuel Beckett . . . two hours into one of his plays you get the first hint of action, a piece of French newspaper blowing across the stage. Two hours later an old tramp farts (he's probably a Sagittarius).

LIBRA MAN – TAURUS WOMAN

Just like the Queen, Taurean women have a lot of 'Tory' in them – no time at all for Libral wimps. And like all Earth signs, they can be very earthy, bound to be disappointed that the only massive Libran erections were created by Christopher Wren.

LIBRA MAN – GEMINI WOMAN

Well, a Libran like Groucho 'Do-you-think-I-could-buy-back-my-introduction-to-you' Marx could be suitably schizophrenic, but many Librans are put off by Gemini's nervous twitches (like winking every time they ask a chemist for a pack of those aspirins).

LIBRA MAN – CANCER WOMAN

The history of Astrology claims that each sign reflects seasonal changes resulting from the Solar orbit. Aries in Spring, being the first Fire sign, the first warmth; Taurus the Earth sign being the Earth *charged* with new life; Gemini, the fertilisation of male and female in plant life; Cancer the Crab, in Summer, symbolising time to go to the seaside. So Cancerian women like beach-boys, not wimps like those indecisive Libran men. Nevertheless, Crabs appeal to Librans like Maggie Thatcher . . . any opportunity to get 'crushed Asians!'

LIBRA MAN – LEO WOMAN

It's no coincidence that the first test-tube baby was born a Leo. Many men are terrified of letting Leo women get hold of their pricks. It's perfectly fitting

99

that the first Olympic games in 776 began on July
23rd, also during Leo. Sex with these women is
always a marathon . . . sometimes a relay, with one
man passing the 'baton' on to the next . . .

LIBRA MAN – VIRGO WOMAN

Remember that Virgos are the people who volunteer
to remove dubious stains in dry cleaners. But they are,
as the name suggests, great liars. Most Virgo c.v.s
detail past experience as 'Company Chairwoman,
Goddess, Olympic Gold Medalist . . .' and they
naturally lie even more about sex. Under Libra Man/
Cancer Woman you'll see how the signs reflect
different seasonal changes throughout the year. After
the summery Leo (time to lie on the beach) comes
Virgo, something that usually gets lost before the end
of the Summer.

LIBRA MAN – LIBRA WOMAN

Libran men just don't know when to get off the fence
with Libran women. It's because they balance their
matronliness on the one hand with rampant
nymphomania on the other. Witness those two
Librans, Sylvia Kristel and Julie Andrews, and the
film, *Emmanuelle Meets Mary Poppins*, full of songs
like 'Feel the birds, tuppence a bang . . .' Libran man
just can't decide which side to go down on. The truth
is, the Sylvia Kristel type will let you go down on both
sides . . .

LIBRA MAN – SCORPIO WOMAN

This is the relationship that could really give Scorpio
woman a Sting in her tail. But in most cases, typically
fair Libran men will loathe the liar that is Scorpio.
After all, Scorpio woman is the perfect advertising
girl, the sort who will describe plastic white 'topping'
as 'Non-Dairy Cream' – anything to distort the truth.
Even a Libran story-teller like Max Bygraves will hate
the sting in their tales. Never buy a second-hand car

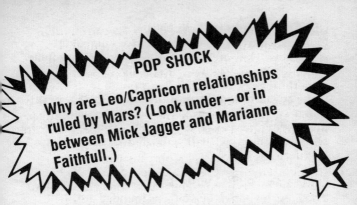

POP SHOCK

Why are Leo/Capricorn relationships ruled by Mars? (Look under – or in between Mick Jagger and Marianne Faithfull.)

from a Scorpio. Never believe that you're 'her first' . . . she's simply forgetting to add 'this evening'.

LIBRA MAN – SAGITTARIUS WOMAN

The world's first heart transplant happened under Sagittarius. It was because someone realised Sagittarians didn't need them. Still, a Libran laugher like Ronnie Barker must have something in common with these old dogs! Sagbags can be outrageously funny. Dirty too. Remember, these are the women with greying bras. Nice people like to think that Sagbags' undies have price tags on because they're new . . . others know better.

LIBRA MAN – CAPRICORN WOMAN

Libran men can be unbearably understanding, like the Judge who lets a hooligan off vandalising a phone-box because he agrees that red can be a pretty heavy colour amongst lovely old stone buildings. These are the Libral wimpoes who promote open prisons and parole, free parking for gays, the ones who can always see the point of view of the coloured person in the woodpile. Capricorn girls are like their male counterparts . . . Idi Amin, Herman Goering, Al Capone, they always see the other person's point of view . . . as wrong!

101

LIBRA MAN – AQUARIUS WOMAN

Libra men are too unbearably fair for outspoken Aquarians. They are the social workers of the zodiac, the ones who say 'I know these kids . . . genocide is something they've just got to get out of their system. Anyway it all stems from being told at the age of three that his grandfather once voted Tory.' Sexually inventive Aquarians, like the Nell Gwynne or Natasha Kinki type, will walk all over these wimps. In stilettoes.

LIBRA MAN – PISCES WOMAN

The French Foreign Legion was founded during Pisces. Most sensible men wish Pisces women would join it. Remember that Librans include Barnes Wallis, inventor of the bomb that could bounce on water. The next day was the birthday of Olivia Neutron-Bomb. 'The Day After' was the birthday of that blonde bombshell Brigitte Bardot *and* also Sylvia Kristel who's forever bouncing up and down. I know this has nothing to do with fish, but by the time you get to the end of writing a book of this length you start realising that every star-sign includes wildly different types of people. The only thing Pisces will find in Astrology is a load of old cod.

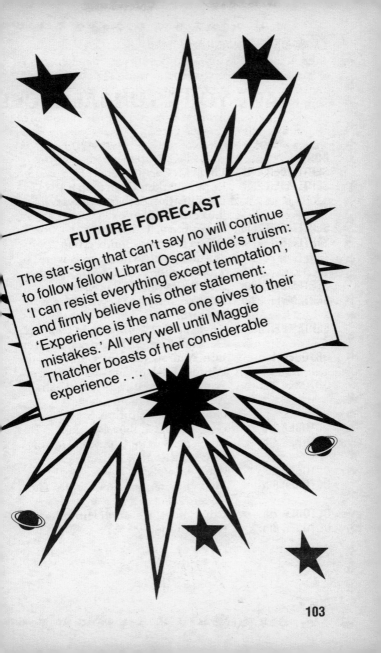

FUTURE FORECAST

The star-sign that can't say no will continue to follow fellow Libran Oscar Wilde's truism: 'I can resist everything except temptation', and firmly believe his other statement: 'Experience is the name one gives to their mistakes.' All very well until Maggie Thatcher boasts of her considerable experience . . .

ARE YOU AS UNBALANCED

BORN:

SEPTEMBER 24th Linda McCartney, Scott Fitzgerald.

SEPTEMBER 25th Ronnie Barker, Christopher Reeve, Leon Brittan, Barbara Walters, 'Luke Skywalker'.

SEPTEMBER 26th Bryan Ferry, T. S. Eliot.

SEPTEMBER 27th Olivia Neutron-Bomb, Alvin Stardust, whose first words were 'Coo-ca-choo', Meat Loaf.

SEPTEMBER 28th Brigitte Bardot, Sylvia Kristel.

SEPTEMBER 29th Seb Coe, Jerry Lee Lewis, Trevor Howard.

SEPTEMBER 30th Angie Dickinson, Truman Capote, Deborah Kerr, Rula Lenska, Radio 1.

OCTOBER 1st Julie Andrews, Jimmy Carter, Walter Matthau, Samuel Beckford.

OCTOBER 2nd Sting, Richard III, Don MacLean, Anna Ford, Graham Greene, Groucho Marx, Jimmy Savile OBE.

OCTOBER 3rd Gore Vidal, Chubby Checker.

OCTOBER 4th Terence Conran, Charlton Heston, Buster Keaton.

OCTOBER 5th Bob Geldof, Donald Pleasanse.

OCTOBER 6th Melvyn Bragg, Barbara Castle, Thor Heyerdahl.

OCTOBER 7th Clive James, Heinrich Himmler.

OCTOBER 8th Ray Reardon.

AS THIS LOT?

OCTOBER 9th	Steve Ovett, Giuseppe Verdi, Donald Sinden, Alastair Sim, John Lennon.
OCTOBER 10th	James Clavell, Harold Pinter, Nicholas Parsons, Midge Ure.
OCTOBER 11th	Bobby Charlton, H. J. Heinz.
OCTOBER 12th	Magnus Magnusson started, Angela Rippon, Luciano Pavarotti.
OCTOBER 13th	MAGGIE THATCHER, Attila the Hun, Adolf Hitler's elder more evil brother, the lead in *Alien*, King Herod, the Devil.
OCTOBER 14th	Roger Moore, Cliff Richard.
OCTOBER 15th	Fergie, Mario Puzo, Roscoe Tanner.
OCTOBER 16th	Peter Bowles, Max Bygraves, Oscar Wilde, Angela Lansbury.
OCTOBER 17th	Evel Knievel, Arthur Miller, Rita Hayworth.
OCTOBER 18th	Martina Navratilova, Chuck Berry.
OCTOBER 19th	Robert Beatty, Bernard Hepton.
OCTOBER 20th	Art Buchwald, Kathy Kirby, Christopher Wren, Ian Rush.
OCTOBER 21st	Leonard Rossiter, Samuel Taylor Coleridge, Julian Cope.
OCTOBER 22nd	Catherine Deneuve, Derek Jacobi, Franz Liszt, Sarah Bernhardt.
OCTOBER 23rd	Johnnie Carson, Pele.

Scorpio

DIRECTIONS FOR

WASP STINGS and OTHER INSECT BITES. For quick relief apply immediately after being stung to the affected area and repeat every 30 minutes

If symptoms persist, consult your Doct Keep out of the reach of children.

SCORPIO

For insect bites, stings & nettle rash.

Bite Cream

THE SIGN OF THE STING IN THE TAIL, (i.e. pain in the arse).

OCTOBER 24th – NOVEMBER 22nd

Fave Pets – slugs.

Scorpios are – everything beginning with '*S*' . . . *silly* like John Cleese; *sparkly* like Su Pollard; *satirical* like Peter Cook; *suspect* like Rock Hudson; *sexy* like Goldie Hawnie; *screwball* like Prince Charles; *secretive* like James Bond; *skilful* like Madonna; *sinful seducers* like Bill Wyman; *shady* like Hank Marvin; *sneaky* like 'Hotlips' Loretta Swit, *swingers* like Gary Player; *stuck-up* and *spoilt* like Tatum O'McEnroe; *systematic* like Marie Curie; *sarcastic* like Gruff Rhys Jones; *starry-eyed* like Edmund Halley; *sinking* like Simon Le Bon; *satanic* like Bram Stoker (author of *Dracula*); *scornful* like Nigel Dempster; *sinister* like Bob Hoskins; *smashing* like Frank Bruno; a *strain* on the ear like Cleo 'the shriek' Laine; *slick* like Henry 'The Fonz' Winkler; *string-pullers* like Jimmy Savile; *showoffs* like Adam Ant; *squat* like Lulu, *strangely-haired* like Art Garfunkel; and otherwise just *smarmy*, *stroppy*, *sly*, *slippery* *scumbags*. The negative Scorpios are considerably worse . . .

More famous Scorpios include – Satan, Beelzebub, The Prince of Darkness, Mephistopheles and the Devil.

Fave children's names – Damien, Carrie.

Typical jobs – freelance embalmer, person who puts pin-pricks in contraceptives (not to be confused with Pisces man: that's just 'pin-size').

OCTOBER 25th – The first publication of the typically Scorpio sardonic magazine *Private Eye*.

OCTOBER 29th – The Wall Street Crash. (Caused by Scorpios characteristically trying to squeeze people dry.)

NOVEMBER 3rd – The first dog in space. Many still wish this had been Scorpio Lulu.

NOVEMBER 4th – The invention of the world's first cash register or 'Jewish piano', a typically Scorpio idea. Scorpios make you pay for everything.

NOVEMBER 14th – What better day than Prince Charles's birthday for another scatty English eccentric to go doing something so spectacularly useful for society as spend all his 'I-want-to-do-barmy-things-like-the-Duke-of-Cornwall-Grant' on discovering the source of the Nile (which in fact turned out to be an early Egyptian carwash.)

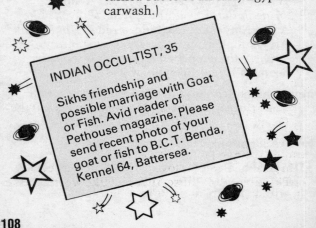

INDIAN OCCULTIST, 35

Sikhs friendship and possible marriage with Goat or Fish. Avid reader of Pethouse magazine. Please send recent photo of your goat or fish to B.C.T. Benda, Kennel 64, Battersea.

All Scorpios behave – as if they're absolutely convinced that their way of doing things is the best way possible. They *all* behave swankily (often without the 's').

THE SCORPIO SALESMAN

All Scorpios have the power to be smarmy salesmen. And whatever they steer you into buying, there's always a catch. These are the men who sell you a low-mileage second-hand car, telling you that of course they haven't wound the mileometer back, but omitting to say that they've put a new one in. These are the estate agents who use phrases such as 'In need of modernisation', meaning it was built before the discovery of cement, or 'full of character', meaning it's got a squatter. This is the travel agent who will promise you a room with an uninterrupted view, but forget to tell you that this only applies if you stick your head out of the window, ignore the wall opposite and look up.

SCORPIO AND SEX

Sadly for sex-mad Scorpios, since the discovery that they all share Rock Hudson's rising sign, membership has been dropping off. Few people want that sort of sting in their tail.

SCORPIO AND DRESS-SENSE

Weird, as anyone who knows a Scorpio will agree. Though Scorpio men hate to see women in trousers, Scorpio Calvin Klein actually 'came out' and designed a range of men's underwear to be worn by women. This is by no means the first time that Scorpio girls have got into men's underwear on a daily basis, simply the first public admission.

In general, Scorpios love dark colours, especially black – unless, of course, they feel like wearing pastel shades or white.

THE BLACK SIDE

Just like the typically Leo Medallion Man, Scorpio men are the ones that buy those black Durex that always embarrass the old ladies or pre-pubescent teenagers who get to serve in chemists. However, whereas Leo men use them to promote their 'Rastus has got nothing on me' image, Scorpios are far more sinister. Wearing black contraceptives, their partners can never see that at least half of what is inside is stuffing.

THE SCORPIO DRIVER

Status-conscious as all Scorpios are, these are the people who queue for hours to ensure that they are the first on their block with the latest car registration plate, and then spend all of August 1st sneakily peering out from behind the lace curtains to see which of the neighbours is feeling most envious. Being such envious creatures themselves, Scorpios love making others jealous.

As regards choice of car, Scorpios love anything they can call 'A sports-'. Anything black and phallic. And they love gadgets. The ultimate Scorpio machine is a black American Transam.

THE STING

The Scorpio's favourite film because it's all about their favourite hobby – revenge. But the famous Scorpio sting in the tail also crops up in other places. For instance, practically everything about a Scorpio will turn out to be less than they led you to believe . . . Especially if you come across the Medallion Man variety. Like Leos, their only charms are on their chunky bracelets, but on closer inspection even the Scorpio bracelets are fakes . . . these are the flash executives who spend all meeting pulling up their cuffs so you can see their gold watches, safe in the knowledge that from your side of the table you can't see that the manufacturer is, in fact, that famous

Taiwan clockmaker 'Lorex'. Look under the table and you'll see that Scorpio's leather loafers are made by 'Yucci'. Those raincoats that look such status symbols from afar are really made by 'Bumberry'. If you follow the Scorpio in the pub wearing a BMW jacket and a Ferrari logo on his jumper, you'll see him drive off in a Ford. If you ever see a Scorpio in a Rolls, he's simply steamed off the hire company's sticker.

SCORPIOS AT HOME
Always stay on the alert. When they offer you Glenfiddich, see if you can spot where they've placed the label over the 'Sainsbury's Whisky' one underneath. These are the people who spend hours decanting supermarket own-label ketchup into Heinz bottles, Tesco marmalade into 'Home-made-labelled' jars. The Sting in the Tail should really read 'stingy'.

HUMOUR SHOCK
Which clown shares the same sign as Spike Milligan, Charlie Chaplin and Chico Marx? (See Michael Heseltine under Aries.)

SCORPIO AT WORK
These sadistic sods are the ones who design Income Tax return forms, the Customs inspectors who delight in your not being able to reseal your suitcase after they've rummaged, the shopkeepers who wait till you're right on their doorstep before turning the door-sign to 'Closed', the bartenders who ignore lunchtime drinkers till 1.30 when they can say, 'I'm sorry, we can't take any more food orders now.'

SCORPIOS AND FUN

Fun for a Scorpio is the classic going into a library and ripping out the final page of whodunnits, (unlike self-pitying Cancerians who only read whodunnits with the last page ripped out). Other Scorpio hobbies include steaming off stamps and applying to be a VAT inspector or traffic warden if they fail their entrance to the SS.

SCORPIO MAN – ARIES WOMAN

Needless to say, any woman will be wary about getting involves with Rock Hudson's rising sign. The only sting in the tail an Aries will put up with is the one they get from a curry; they love hot food. In most cases, a Scorpio man won't be enough to satisfy an Arietian girl's rapacious appetite, and he'll only get wildly jealous when she attracts other admirers. Remember, Aries is the Fire sign that is permanently on heat.

SCORPIO MAN – TAURUS WOMAN

He's far too much of a spiv for this down to Earth Mother. Whilst she'll prefer driving a staid Rover, Volvo or tractor, Scorpio men are those twits in cravates commonly known as Triumph Spitfire pilots. A girl who likes sex to be as straightforward as a Taurean will hate Scorpio's obsession with putting go-fast stripes down his durex.

SCORPIO MAN – GEMINI WOMAN – GEMINI WOMAN

Yes, it can happen. Remember, sex with a Gemini is like a threesome, and the sign of Joan Collins is certainly into variety. And most Scorpio men like to regard themselves as walking sex manuals, though they get very jealous. Scorpio man/Gemini woman/Gemini woman would be good for a one-night stand provided both or all involved are too drunk to remember names the next day.

112

SCORPIO MAN – CANCER WOMAN

A right royal cock-up. This is the Prince Charles/Lady Di relationship. Ask yourself if you've got anything in common with them? Is *she* like a cancer on your savings? Does *he* hold lengthy conversations with trees? Does *she* see as much real life as fellow sign Helen Keller? Or think Princes can still behave the way they do in the novelettes of that other Crabby old relative, Barbara Cartland? Beware, Scorpio, once a Crab gets her claws into your 'crown jewels', you'll be emasculated forever. You might as well call yourself a Pisces. This is also the John Cleese/Prunella Scales relationship. Guests in their house will always be treated as obstacles.

SCORPIO MAN – LEO WOMAN

Beware the Lion's den. Only the slyest Scorpios will survive the sauciness of Lionesses like Mata Hari or Madonna. Remember that Leo man can be just as much of a lounge lizard as Scorpio. And it's just the same with the women. Like Leo Mae West, these women are all front. And they won't like it when sneaky Scorpios like Nigel Dempster try to show them up. In fact, Leos like Princess Margaret firmly maintain that that particular Scorpio doesn't have a dustbin; he simply puts everything straight into print.

SCORPIO MAN – VIRGO WOMAN

No way. Charming and skilfully seductive as all Scorpios like to think they are, every girl who loves good clean fun is going to be repulsed by that sign saying Turbo on Scorpio's underpants. Splashing on another gallon of Denim aftershave won't do the trick either. There's not much hope for a relationship where both partners are continually suspicious and critical of the other, and, let's face it, when a girl like Raquel Welch tells you she's a Virgo, you're bound to want to ask questions.

★ SCORPIO MAN – LIBRA WOMAN

As a rule, Libran ladies are unimpressed by lounge lizards. So that flashy trick of yours of stopping every telephone call with 'I'll have to call you back, we're just entering a tunnel,' won't work. Librans like class, not the sort of playboy who drives around town in a Condom GTI, telling all the girls he's got an even bigger five-speed gearstick in the bedroom. Politically it would be stalemate too. Can you see Libran Thatcher getting anything other than questions from Scorpio Sir Robin Day, or him getting any answers from her? Even on a Scorpio's high slyness rating, most Librans go off the scales . . .

★ SCORPIO MAN – SCORPIO WOMAN

Permanently trying to out-trick the other, and the women usually win. Remember, Scorpio checkout girls in supermarkets are the ones who always let you unload your trolley before announcing that they're just off to lunch.

☆ SCORPIO MAN – SAGITTARIUS WOMAN

Well, he'll have no trouble in getting his wicked way. Sagbags find 'No' an unusually long word to have to pronounce. But will he be happy? Very unlikely. Sexy as Tina Turner and her fellow star signs may appear up on stage, Sagittarians have very dubious personal habits, like putting roll-on deodorants under their arms *after* they've put their blouses on – and that's only to disguise the fact that the garment's never been washed. No, Sagbags are not only dirty in the way you'd like them to be. Witness Sagittarian **B. O.** Derek.

SCORPIO MAN – CAPRICORN WOMAN

Scorpios may be stingy, but never as stingy as those tight-fisted Goats. The most generous Capricorn ever was Scrooge. If you ever get a Christmas card from a Capricorn you will notice a list of names crossed out in front of yours and instructions to cross out your own and post it on to the people below. And they all think they're God. They all like to be sent birthday cards at Christmas.

SCORPIO MAN – AQUARIUS WOMAN

Nell Gwynne, Zsa Zsa Gabor, Princess Caroline . . . all the attractive ones can twist men round their little fingers. As for the rest . . . Virginia Woolf, Germaine Greer, Vanessa Redgrave, they'll all hate Scorpio's right-wing tendencies . . . that little black moustache will have to go. And the armband. And the jackboots. The only successful Scorpio Man/Aquarius Woman relationship was James Bond with Lois 'Moneypenny' Maxwell. Be as secretive as you like, Scorpio, she'll always know what you're up to. But she'll never satisfy your demands to be called 'Thunderballs'.

SCORPIO MAN – PISCES WOMAN

Even serious astrologers say that Scorpio men drink like fish. It's a good job, if they want to keep up with Pisceans. This is the Richard Burton/Liz Taylor relationship. But is your Pisces lady as slippery and hard to get hold of as a fish? Like Liz do you have to marry her at least three times to be sure she's yours? Pisces women want all their dreams to come true, and when they do, they're not dreams anymore. Like a Sagittarian in bed, these girls are a 'nightmare'.

FUTURE FORECAST

In the coming year, swanky Scorpios will continue to collect foreign carrier bags to provide international street-cred status when they get home.

Stingy Scorpios will simply get a friend to collect the bags on their behalf, and meanwhile post several cards back home under their name to make the trip look convincing.

DO YOU STING AS

BORN:

OCTOBER 24th	Bill Wyman, Sir Robin Day.
OCTOBER 25th	Chaucer, the first *Private Eye*, Helen Reddy.
OCTOBER 26th	Jaclyn Smith, Bob Hoskins, François Mitterand.
OCTOBER 27th	John Cleese, Roy Lichtenstein, Captain Cooke, Erasmus, Simon le Bon.
OCTOBER 28th	Cleo Laine, Hank Marvin, Francis Bacon.
OCTOBER 29th	Richard Dreyfuss, Robert Hardy.
OCTOBER 30th	Henry 'The Fonz' Winkler, Ezra Pound, Richard Brinsley Sheridan, Diego Maradonna.
OCTOBER 31st	Dick Francis, Jimmy Savile.
NOVEMBER 1st	Nigel Dempster, Gary Player, E.R.N.I.E.
NOVEMBER 2nd	Burt Lancaster, Marie Antoinette.
NOVEMBER 3rd	Adam Ant, Charles Bronson, Ludovic Kennedy, Viscount Linley, Lulu.
NOVEMBER 4th	Loretta Swit, Walter Cronkite.
NOVEMBER 5th	Tatum O'Neal, Art Garfunkel, Lester Piggott, Roy Rogers.
NOVEMBER 6th	Donald Houston, P.J. Proby.

MUCH AS THIS LOT?

NOVEMBER 7th	Jean Shrimpton, Marie Curie, Su Pollard.
NOVEMBER 8th	Ken Dodd, Margaret Mitchell, Bram Stoker.
NOVEMBER 9th	Katharine Hepburn, the first *Young Ones* (1982).
NOVEMBER 10th	Richard Burton, Tim Rice.
NOVEMBER 11th	Roy Jenkins, June Whitfield.
NOVEMBER 12th	Neil Young, Auguste Rodin.
NOVEMBER 13th	Robert Louis Stevenson.
NOVEMBER 14th	Prince Charles, Muffin the Mule.
NOVEMBER 15th	Peter Phillips (son of Princess Anne and the pillock).
NOVEMBER 16th	Griff Rhys Jones, Tiberius, Frank Bruno.
NOVEMBER 17th	Peter Cook, Rock Hudson, Fenella Fielding.
NOVEMBER 18th	Kim Wilde, David Hemmings, Linda Evans.
NOVEMBER 19th	Jodie Foster, Calvin Klein, Indira Gandhi.
NOVEMBER 20th	Alastair Cooke.
NOVEMBER 21st	Goldie Hawn, Harpo Marx, René Magritte.
NOVEMBER 22nd	Billie Jean King, Tom Conti, Terry Gilliam, George Eliot.

Sagittarius

SIGN OF THE HALF-HUMAN
NOVEMBER 23rd – DECEMBER 21st

People who are at least 50% wild animal – Ian Botham, Boris Karloff, General Franco, Tina Turner, Mel Smith, Bette Midler.

More popular Centaurs – Leisure Centaurs, Cine-Centaurs, Woody Allen, Churchill, Frank Sinatra, Bo Derek, Steven Spielberg, Jane Fonda (born during a triple backswing on the cusp).

Famous Italian stallions – The Emperor 'Nero', Hengist & Horsa, Larry 'the limb' Uppafilli, Tossonaponi.

Famous Sagittarian benders – Uri Geller, Lionel Blair.

Typical Sagittarians love – horsing around, having a nag (often literally), being tactless, dressing sloppily, getting their oats on a daily basis.

Typical jobs include – rear end of pantomime horse, person who stuffs animals (or vice versa), anything in the cavalry, person who conducts Gallup polls.

Number of teeth – 52 (most apparent on Sagittarian women, who tend to be Sloaney in the extreme).

Fave radio show – *The Archers*.

Fave Club – Derby & Joan.

Fave cars – Citroën Deux Chevaux or Golf G-GTI.

Least favourite film – *The Godfather*.

Least favourite food – horse d'oeuvres.

Least favourite singer – Maurice Chevalier.

STAR SHOCK

Which 'British Open' began on John Newcombe's birthday? (See Joan Collins under Gemini.)

Typical Sagittarians are – lousy at keeping a tight rein on spending, bestial in bed, clumsy, accident prone.

Sagittarius and sex – just like horses, they all adore being mounted, and it's amazing what you can do with 'sixteen hands'. Fave sexual variation: fillyatio . . .

Dubious personal habits – in one way or another, they are all filthy. You can always recognize a Sagittarian man by the dribbles down his trouser-fronts. This is simply because, after peeing in a public place, the clumsy oaf is either too lazy to shake himself dry or else worried that by doing so other people will think he's indulging in a Piscean favourite hobby.

   The women are just as bad. Sagittarian mothers are the ones who yell to their children, 'Make sure you've got your underpants on the right way round . . . yellow at the front, brown at the back!'

Fave Sagittarius pet – skunk, something they feel will bring a breath of fresh air into their homes.

The sharpest Sagittarian dresser – 'Worzel Gummidge'.

THE STALLIONS

Yes, that's how Sagittarian men like to think of themselves. Just like thoroughbred horses, getting their oats every day and always having a 'bit' on the side. The truth is more like Sagittarian Ian Botham, the so-called stud who's generally out to grass. However much a sporty Sagittarian loves his lads' nights out, he's far too clumsy to bowl a maiden over (unless she's a similarly basic Filly). Scoring on grass, of either variety, is one thing . . . but for Sagittarian man to score with women with brains or morals, it's a tough match. The problem is basically that Sagittarian man is generally the outdoor type; people like to keep them outdoors because they're so raucous and clumsy. If it's not for their hearty horseplay, it's because, like Sagittarian Woody Allen, this sign can be a nervous wreck, guaranteed to drop any precious vase you give them to hold. Always breaking the most valuable glasses when washing up . . . any knobs they try out in your new car always snap off. It's simply because they're paranoid. And wouldn't you be if your birth sign showed the back end of a horse stuffed up the front end of a man? Imagine Woody Allen having nightmares every night that he's being raped by a stallion . . . this is true Sagittarian man. No wonder he's terrified of stable relationships . . . no wonder he never visits masseuses advertised as 'black beauty' . . . and no wonder anyone who's ever had a Sagittarian lover will have been subjected to everything they never wanted to know about sex – jockey shorts are just the beginning, wait till he tries to whip up your enthusiasm . . . Sagittarian men even breed horses – look at the Aga Khan. They're a very strange breed themselves, especially the really crazy Horses like Donny Osmond, the man who put **a git** in **Sagit**tarius. What other sign would make a record about a boy falling in love with a puppy while all the normal kids had girlfriends? It's back to bestiality, like Woody Allen and that sheep in the film . . .

Sagittarian men even like being called horsey names. Look at Winston 'Whinny' Churchill. Unless you love the sort of man who tactlessly charges into everything, falling for a Sagittarian is what Churchill called the beginning of the end . . . a randy stallion will never surrender.

Home for Mr Sagittarius will be full of horse brasses, anything to remind him of the pub. If he's sporty, as they often are, he'll have his trophies alongside, or an old bat (i.e. the wife). However much these archers fancy themselves as beaux, they rarely attract decent women for long. And it's hardly surprising – they're either the raucous hearties cracking jokes like, 'I thought a horse chestnut was something a tart had under her bra,' or else the paranoid type like Woody Allen, constantly terrified that their wives might leave them for another woman . . . is this really what you want? The Botham-type Sagittarian, who attracts women who are also half-whores? Or the neurosis collector who worries that he's getting penis envy?

POP SHOCK

Why are Cancerians so often associated with things wet? (See George Michael under Cancer and Drips.)

THE FILLIES

If anyone's horsey it's Sagittarian women, or 'gels' as
these Sloaney types like to be called. They've
generally got far too many teeth, displayed through
vast smiles plus pony-tails, scarves with horses on
and a positively determined stride to their step.
There's rarely anything very feminine about these
tomboys. They're strapping lasses, like Sagittarian
Bette Midler, tactless as hell, charging out with wild
abuse, unshockable as Pamela Stephenson, or bestial
as Tina Turner. They've all got huge, powerful
mouths. As for everything being 'in the best possible
taste' . . . no way. This girl is one of the lads —
strident, stroppy and strictly for fun. All the best
striptease artistes are Sagittarians, many of them
women too. Yes, you can get a Filly to perform all
sorts; they love to be on stage and entertaining. Mind
you, they hate cooking, especially if they have to do
it. Junk food and anything instant is okay by them.
And who cares about sitting down and being formal?
Sagittarian women don't care if anyone sneers at
them for eating in the street, or on the pavement. If
anyone dares to reprimand Ms Centaur, she'll get on
her high horse immediately, and put on all the snooty
airs of Sagittarians like Christina Onassis or that old
groomer, Lucie Clayton, playing up the Sloane Ranger
bit to the full. And when they're not being Rangerish
or raunchey, they're ranchy, like the poison dwarf
cowgirl, 'Lucy' from *Dallas*. Yes, Charlene Tilton
really is a Sagittarian, in fact the only one who never

sticks her neck out . . . though there have been other little women before her, like Louisa M. Alcott, who also wrote *Little Men*, which no doubt included Sagittarian Ronnie Corbett, who once described himself as 'a hitman for the Brownies'. And all good Sagittarian 'gels' join the Brownies and the pony club. If they grow up, they join the hunt. And in everything, it's Sagittarian women who do the chasing, galloping round town in provocative Tina Turner outfits, being outrageous. If you're not into leather jodhpurs and whips, don't get saddled with a Sagittarian . . . they can be like nuns with your friends, like saints in the office and (w)horse in bed. If you're not into animal passion, a Sagittarian after dark can be a 'nightmare . . .'

SEX SHOCK

Did you know that Richard III shares a sign with history's other most famous humper? (See Sylvia Kristel under Libra.)

SAGITTARIUS MAN – ARIES WOMAN

The more idealistic Sagittarian man like Churchill or Blake will find any Ram far too woolly. Remember, the sign of the rampant is only really concerned with things physical, they barely know what a brain is. But even a Ram will find Sagittarian man too tactless and outspoken. These are the Ian Bothams of the world, the outspoken oafs who do things like march into a parachute brigade's mess and announce that they thought only fairies had wings. Unless she likes people who start fights, an Aries woman will simply use a Sagittarian man for keeping her rose-bed well fertilised.

SAGITTARIUS MAN – TAURUS WOMAN

The typical farmer's wife type of woman could well appreciate a Sagman around the place. After all, she'll make good use of the fact that he leaves far bigger droppings than all the other signs. The only problem being when she realises that it comes out of his mouth as well, and she's full of Bull herself. Still, Sagittarian men like Ian Botham can always get jobs as muck-spreaders . . . in the *Sun* – the *Star*, 'The News of the Screws' . . .

SAGITTARIUS MAN – GEMINI WOMAN

Infinitely more refined Gemini woman is hardly going to settle for the Botham brigade of Sagittarian bum-scratchers and bogey-flickers, but the Woody Allen variety may provide just what her dual personality is looking for. In fact only a many-faceted double-act like the Twins could cope with his paranoia. And a Sagittarian hypochondriac/neurotic/ paranoid like Woody will find no solace whatsoever in any sign less schizo than Gemini. 'I hope I'm ill,' he will say. 'Why?' she will reply. 'Because I'd hate to feel this bad and be well,' he says. Only a Gemini could cope with that.

SAGITTARIUS MAN – CANCER WOMAN

Anyone as mixed up as the Woody Allen breed of Sagittarian will find greedy Cancerians unbearable in the way they have to get their claws into everything, and childish too, especially over things to do with water. Wasn't it Woody Allen who detested his wife for being so childish she even burst in on him when he was in the bathroom and sank all his ships and ducks . . .

SAGITTARIUS MAN – LEO WOMAN

Even the wildest animals, which Leos certainly are, will hate a man whose favourite hobby is taxidermy, particularly when he's so sloppy about his personal habits. Remember, Sagittarian men only know when they last washed their underwear by sniffing it. They're also the outspoken oafs who make loud comments in restaurants when other people are served before them, or complain raucously if anyone ahead of them in a supermarket queue dares to bring out a cheque-book . . . far too common for the pride of lions.

SAGITTARIUS MAN – VIRGO WOMAN

Well old farty-breath isn't going to get far with Miss Spotless. Most Sagittarian men only introduce themselves after intercourse. Virgoans like their men to have the same ridiculously trim beards as Virgo men; Sagittarians just have what is best described as face fungus – the men are even worse. No, the only possible pairing is Virgoan Raquel Welch in her *One Million Years B.C.* role. She'd get on well with Sagittarians, 'The Neanderthals of the Zodiac'.

SAGITTARIUS MAN – LIBRA WOMAN

Far too chauvinistic a man for the Thatcher brigade. Idealists like Churchill will more than meet their match. Librans can weigh down very heavily on anyone who doesn't give into them. There are a few slightly less heavy-going examples, like folk singer Julie Felix, but when she sang 'Daddy's Taking Us To the Zoo Tomorrow', she meant that Daddy was taking them as inmates not visitors. Get involved with the sign of Thatcher and you too will wish your Libra had a cage.

SAGITTARIUS MAN – SCORPIO WOMAN

Whether you're the raucous oaf type of Sagittarian like Botham or the nervy paranoid like Woody Allen, every Sagittarian man feels that people are getting at him unfairly, and if anyone enjoys playing around with people's feelings it's a Scorpio woman. Just to show you how sadistic they can be, it was a Scorpio woman who designed the unwrappable silver paper on triangles of cheese spread.

SAGITTARIUS MAN – SAGITTARIUS WOMAN

The Billy Connolly/Pamela Stephenson relationship. He of the wild face fungus and she of the big mouth. These two will love each other's outrageous sense of humour. They are instantly compatible, and will remain so as long as both stay rich, successful, charming and randy. Otherwise it's D.I.V.O.R.C.E.

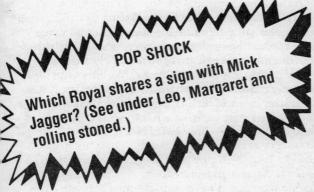

POP SHOCK

Which Royal shares a sign with Mick Jagger? (See under Leo, Margaret and rolling stoned.)

SAGITTARIUS MAN – CAPRICORN WOMAN

Sagittarian man is nearly as subtle as a fart in a crowded lift. Capricorns are very demanding, and *very* proper. Hardly likely to approve of the way the Botham brigade take such delight in rubbing their balls on their trousers in public. To bowl one of these maidens over, Sagman would have to brush up his manners considerably . . . especially in bed. The Botham brigade still think a woman only gets a cap if she's had sex for England. This is the Woody Allen/Diane Keaton pairing too. How many neuroses have you got in common with them? (Use the four spare pages at the back for notes.)

SAGITTARIUS MAN – AQUARIUS WOMAN

You have to understand that the most modern-thinking Sagittarian man was Fred Flintstone. Aquarian women of the Germaine Greer variety are hardly going to be impressed with the man who thinks women's libbers don't mind if you rip their bras off. Subtle hints like 'Feminists are just women who are too ugly to get a man' never really go down that well either. The Botham boys may think they're outstanding in their field. Aquarian women wish they were out standing in their field.

SAGITTARIUS MAN – PISCES WOMAN

Sea-horses are a very rare breed indeed. And when you do get 'white horses' on the water, it's usually the sign of a storm or excessive wind, a Sagittarian problem that few find endearing. No, this is an unlikely match. Sagittarians like action. Pisces love dreaming about it. Tell them to get their skates on and they all start wearing what look like live codpieces. Far too slippery for Horses.

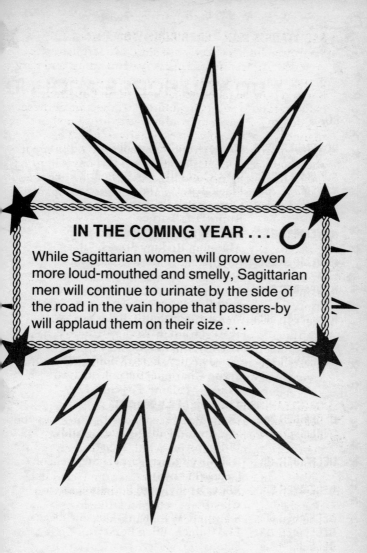

IN THE COMING YEAR . . .

While Sagittarian women will grow even more loud-mouthed and smelly, Sagittarian men will continue to urinate by the side of the road in the vain hope that passers-by will applaud them on their size . . .

DO YOU HORSE AROUND

BORN:

NOVEMBER 23rd	Champion the Wonderhorse, Boris Karloff, the first *Dr Who*.
NOVEMBER 24th	Billy Connolly, Ian Botham, Trigger.
NOVEMBER 25th	Black Beauty, *The Mousetrap*.
NOVEMBER 26th	Charles Schulz, Pat Phoenix, Red Rum, Tina Turner.
NOVEMBER 27th	Ernie Wise, Jimi Hendrix, John Alderton, Rodney Bewes, Silver.
NOVEMBER 28th	Randy Newman, William Blake, Nancy Mitford, Pegasus.
NOVEMBER 29th	Louisa M. Alcott, most Shetland ponies.
NOVEMBER 30th	Winston Churchill, Jonathan Swift, Mark Twain, Robert Vaughan, Gary Lineker, Billy Idol.
DECEMBER 1st	Woody Allen, Bette Midler, Richard Pryor, Charlene 'the poison dwarf' Tilton, Madame Tussaud, Lee Travino, Mary Martin.
DECEMBER 2nd	General Haig.
DECEMBER 3rd	Mel Smith, Paul Nicholas, Andy Williams.
DECEMBER 4th	Ronnie Corbett, Pamela Stephenson, General Franco.
DECEMBER 5th	Walt Disney, Lord Longford, Lucie Clayton.
DECEMBER 6th	Jonathan 'Wan' King, Dave Brubeck.
DECEMBER 7th	Eli Wallach, Ellen Burstyn.
DECEMBER 8th	Sammy Davis Jr, Mary Queen of

AS MUCH AS THIS LOT?

	Scots, James Thurber.
DECEMBER 9th	*Coronation Street*, Donny Osmond, Kirk Douglas, Judi Dench, Joan Armatrading.
DECEMBER 10th	Dorothy Lamour.
DECEMBER 11th	Christina Onassis, Alexander Solzhenitsyn.
DECEMBER 12th	Tracey Austin, Lionel Blair, Frank Sinatra, Dionne Warwick, Emmerson Fittipaldi, John Osborne.
DECEMBER 13th	Jim Davidson, the Aga Khan, George Schultz.
DECEMBER 14th	Lee Remick, Stan Smith, Nostradamus (who predicted his own birth).
DECEMBER 15th	John Paul Getty, Edna O'Brien, Nero.
DECEMBER 16th	Arthur C. Clarke, Liv Ullman, Noel Coward.
DECEMBER 17th	Bernard Hill, Simon Bates, Tommy Steel.
DECEMBER 18th	Steven Spielberg, Keith Richards, Charles Wesley.
DECEMBER 19th	Eamon Andrews 'this-is-your-birthday,' Edith Piaf, Gordon Andrews, Ralph Richardson, Leonid Brezhnev.
DECEMBER 20th	Bo Derek, Jenny Agutter, Uri Geller, Geoffrey Howe.
DECEMBER 21st	Chris Evert-Lloyd, Joseph Stalin, Frank Zappa and Jane Fonda (born during a triple back swing).

Capricorn

THE PEOPLE WHO GET ON YOUR GOAT.
DECEMBER 22nd – JANUARY 20th.

Famous goats include – Billy the Kid, David Bowie, Elvis Presley, Rod Stewart, Al Capone, Idi Amin, Diane Keaton, Matt Frewer (alias Max Headroom), Victoria Principal and Jesus Christ (most Capricorns reckon His dad is one too).

Typical Capricorn jobs – Nanny, Messiah, Legend, Dictator.

Capricorns will happily admit to being – capricious, ambitious, determined, on the same wavelength as God.

Their basic fault – despite their apparent wit, most Capricorns are pretty suspect, i.e. take away the **C——orn**, and you're left with **—apric——**!

Capricorns call their children – 'Zowie', 'Hound-dog', 'Omnipotent one'

AND IT CAME TO PASS . . .

That God created a tight-fisted bastard called Capricorn. Even Jesus fitted the description. He only got the nickname 'King of the Jews' after making five thousand guests sit down to a lunch of just five fishes and two loaves. Ever since, Capricorns have been recognised as eternal bargain-hunters . . .

THE CAPRICORN IN HIS CAR . . .

These are the mean sods who will drive round and round for miles trying to find a cheaper petrol station. They will gloat as all Goats do when they can tell you that they paid 2p a gallon less than you did in the local garage, omitting to say that this was only because of a two hundred mile round trip.

AT HOME

They are stingier still. Greedy Capricorns linger longest in the pub so they can go round finishing everybody's drinks. After parties, Capricorns will surreptitiously pour what's left in people's glasses back into the bottles from whence they came. When invited to Bring a Bottle parties, these are the guests who always take cider and quickly bury it amongst the host of other bottles before anyone notices. Many Capricorn hosts even dilute their guests' water.

THE CAPRICORN MUM

One mean mother. Many have been known to make their children sift through their own sick to find undigested 'greens' that can be squeezed for vitamins at a later date. *Never ever* accept 'soup of the house' in a Capricorn kitchen!

DUBIOUS HABITS

If you consider hanging the loo paper out to dry a dubious habit, then Capricorns are pretty dubious. Many Capricorn mothers put name tags on their children's loo paper.

THEY WEAR

Anything on which they can negotiate for discount in Oxfam. Remember, these are the people who wanted to know when Band Aid were having a sale.

MILKING EVERY LAST DROP

Whereas hygienic Virgos always sniff the milk to tell if it's fresh, Capricorns sniff milk because they don't want to fork out on anything dearer. Due to the price of bottled milk, most Capricorn mothers breast feed until their children are old enough to leave home.

TELL-TALE SIGNS

A badge saying, 'Hello, I'm a Capricorn'; a woman wearing yesterday's make-up; a company chairman who still lets his mother choose his clothes and therefore turns up to board meetings in a romper suit

STAR SHOCK

Yes, Aquarians really are the people to whom you can say 'Your movements are ruled by Uranus'. Not surprisingly, they include Ronald Reagan.

and nappies. Whereas Sagittarian women simply regard holes in tights as providing easier access, Capricorn women are the ones who go round filling in laddered black stockings with felt tip to save buying new ones. Capricorn men hardly take any time at all to go to the loo. They rarely spend a penny, usually a half-penny.

CAPRICORN AND SEX
The sight of all those sheaths and caps hanging out to dry on the Capricorn washing line usually prevents new partners from ever getting this far. Sex with a Capricorn can be a real pain – that even includes Cynthia Payne! Nobody bothers dressing up for *her* Vicars 'n' Tart parties . . .

GREAT CAPRICORN WAYS OF RELAXING . . .

1.

2.

3.

4.

5.

6.

7.

8.

9.

10.

GREAT CAPRICORN WAYS OF FORGETTING ABOUT WORK . . .

1.

2.

3.

4.

5.

6.

7.

8.

HOW WELL DO YOU KNOW YOUR CAPRICORN PARTNER?

1: Do you know their name?

2: At exhibitions and shows, do they still amass every colour brochure that's free and sell them to friends who couldn't go?

3: Do they waste time over trifles? Or ice-cream?

4: Do they like to be called 'mighty one' or 'Hosanna'?

5: If he/she/it was given too much change would your Capricorn partner go back to the shop and say he/she/it had been overcharged?

6: Does he/she/it believe in equality for all workers?

7: Is life an important factor in their career?

CAPRICORN MAN ON HIGH

This can take on all sorts of different significances depending on whether you're considering the Jesus Christ variety of Capricorn or the David Bowie kind . . . what is certain is that once they get to the top, most Capricorns see themselves as God. The most positive one insisting that his prayers end with Amen, the most negative, dictating that everything ends with Amin. *Note*: Muhammed Ali, 'I am the greatest'; Jesus, 'I am the way'; Idi Amin, 'I is dee way'.

Life for Capricorn man is never normal or mediocre. He's either the king who's climbed to the top, like Elvis, Bowie, Rod Stewart, Al Capone or Howard Hughes, or else he's the king for whom life will always be the pits, like 'King' Arthur Scargill. Other Capricorn kings include Martin Luther King and Nat King Cole. But none of them are merry old souls; all the time they spend getting to the top will see them head down, determined and never switching off from work. And once they get there, the permanent frustration of where to go next sets in. It's practically impossible for Capricorn man to define 'enough'. Even J.C. could well have said, as studio boss Sam Goldwyn proclaimed whilst filming *The Last Supper*, 'Why only twelve? Go out and get thousands.' Though Capricorns hate spending their own hard-earned money. And they can save like Cancerians by being every bit as sneaky as Scorpios. For instance, you will never find a Capricorn paying for his TV or video; he will simply borrow it on one month's free trial from the store and when the month is up, move on to the next store. They are just as resourceful as they are methodical. But there's madness in their method, like David Bowie, 'A lad insane . . .'

STAR SHOCK

Words often associated with Crabs: nasty rash, itching, clinic, pain when pee-ing.

CAPRICORN WOMAN

Many astrologers claim Capricorn women get to the top of the mountain because they are great social climbers. How can this possibly be true of the star-sign of Princess Michael? Many also claim that Capricorn girls have more than the occasional drink when they are unhappy. How can this be true of the star-sign that includes Janis Joplin?

But one thing is certain; even if these complex, ambitious creatures overcome being depressed by the mountain of tasks they always set themselves, they certainly provide a mountain for others to climb. (In Victoria Principal's case we are talking twin peaks). Capricorn girls get quickly uninterested in anyone or anything that fails to come up to their high expectations. Financially, ambitiously, mentally, socially, whatever. Most Capricorn girls see the world from a high position: Janet Street-Porter – because she's well over six foot, Princess Michael's nearly as tall, as is Maggie Smith and Donna Summer. Faye Dunaway's just as commanding. Yes, Capricorn girls find it very easy to look down on others (well, Victoria Principal doesn't, most things below her chest level still remain a mystery . . .)

Miserly, sadistic, unfeeling, cruel bastards. These are not nice words. Let's just say, nice Capricorns have tight-fisted, damning tendencies. And they are never easy to understand. Just take Diane Keaton as a typical example. Unlike Sagittarians, Capricorn girls are rarely won over by chat-up lines such as 'Mine's a whopper, luv!' They expect you to pass all sorts of mental tests on top, and even then, no partner will ever fully measure up to their own standards or expectations.

Physically, they are generally tall and thin. Except for the short, flabby ones.

They're not really as snobby as people make out; they just despise people that shop in supermarkets . . . And they can be very bitchy. Capricorn comedienne Joan Rivers said that someone she knows had been a tart all her life; she'd even had a red light outside her doll's house. When she got married, she couldn't say who the best man was until she'd tried them all . . .

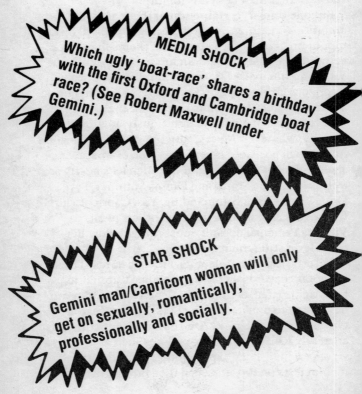

MEDIA SHOCK

Which ugly 'boat-race' shares a birthday with the first Oxford and Cambridge boat race? (See Robert Maxwell under Gemini.)

STAR SHOCK

Gemini man/Capricorn woman will only get on sexually, romantically, professionally and socially.

CAPRICORN MAN – ARIES WOMAN

Is any woman really going to be good enough or God enough for the sign that includes Jesus? It won't be libidinous Aries, that's for sure; these girls never like waiting long for the second coming . . . Like the Royal Air Force (appropriately founded under Aries) plodding Capricorns will find Aries girls far too up in the air and flighty. The only possible pairing is with negative Capricorn Idi Amin . . . head in the clouds, high as a kite and taking off with any woman that came along.

CAPRICORN MAN – TAURUS WOMAN

Well, J.C. is hardly going to approve of any Cow who wants to be considered sacred . . . and don't forget that it was on May 4th, under Taurus that Britain received her first *Daily Mail*. Taurean women who are heavily into a bit of the udder, need their daily male. They should stick to Capricorns of the Cary Grant and Rod Stewart variety, the ones most women generally find hard in bed.

CAPRICORN MAN – GEMINI WOMAN

Don't forget that Gemini is the sign of Joan Collins. Who could possibly have any respect for the woman who married the only Scandinavian with less sex appeal than the 'Swedish Chef'? Besides, the more prudish Capricorn is bound to point out that even on D-Day which happened during Gemini, far less Americans landed in France than the number that have landed on certain Gemini women . . .

CAPRICORN MAN – CANCER WOMAN

The very first British National Cat Show happened on July 13th, during Cancer. It featured many Cancerian women. Catty, crabby, it's hard to believe there really is a softie inside that tough shell. Unlike Capricorn J.C., Cancerian women are typically as unforgiving as their archetype, Prunella Scales in her 'Sybil Fawlty' role, affectionately dubbed 'my little Piranha' by Basil.

CAPRICORN MAN – LEO WOMAN

How's a holier than thou Capricorn going to react to a lusty Leo like Mae West? Just picture Jesus being asked, 'Is that a crucifix in your pocket, or are you just pleased to see me?' On the other-hand, Capricorns like J. R. R. Tolkien love anything that comes in massive volumes, so Leo girls could be on . . . but definitely not with the Jesus brigade. Mary Magdalene was a Leo. J.C. only had that bloody great boulder put over his door because he was terrified as to what old lusty might do to him while he was asleep.

CAPRICORN MAN – VIRGO WOMAN

One famous astrologer said that a Virgo woman will love the way a Capricorn man 'can make her do things she never thought possible.' In J.C.'s case this probably means raising from the dead, walking on water, a whole load of fun. Hygienic Virgo will also love the way he doesn't hang around with slobs . . . all his best mates are saints. But Virgos do like to move on, to let bygones be bygones . . . she'll get very upset when you say you're dead, then pop back for a few days, only to zoom up into a position from which you can judge her until eternity.

CAPRICORN MAN – LIBRA WOMAN

Well, it's not going to work trying to balance Librans like Thatcher with the Messiah variety of Capricorn.

'Fair's fair,' she'll say. 'They've had a man sitting on God's right hand for long enough – it's high time they had a woman . . . come to think of it, why don't you sit on my right hand? I thought Jeffrey Archer was going to be a string-puller, but think what economic miracles I could perform with you . . .' Libran women are very attracted to the sort who are all forgiveness. Most offers they get are from devils. Still, a negative Capricorn like Idi Amin would probably see eye to eye with her on most things; he's just as diplomatic. But even ferocious black men are no match for Maggie. Even 'Mr T' is less ferocious than Mrs T.

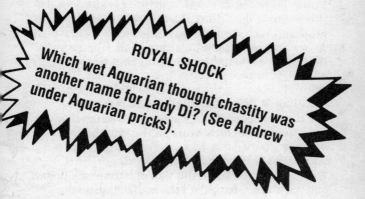

ROYAL SHOCK

Which wet Aquarian thought chastity was another name for Lady Di? (See Andrew under Aquarian pricks).

CAPRICORN MAN – SCORPIO WOMAN

Date a Scorpio girl and you'll soon see why Borstal was genuinely created during Scorpio. Nobody misbehaves more. Look at Scorpio woman George Eliot becoming famous by pretending to be a man . . . rather like Scorpio Prince Charles. 'Charlie's Angel' Jaclyn Smith is also a Scorpio, and just the type who'd hate the sting a Capricorn might give in her tail end. You see, though they are not 'do-it-yourself' sex experts like Pisceans, many Capricorns still believe that a man can't have a good solid screw without first inserting a rawl plug.

CAPRICORN MAN – SAGITTARIUS WOMAN

She's one of the few signs that make this gloomy old bugger laugh, something even a Capricorn miracle-worker like Jesus could not do . . . where's it say in the Bible, 'And it came to pass that our Lord had a good old giggle.'. . ? There he was, having supper with twelve of his best mates, and not one of them told a joke – not one of them invents '101 Uses For A Dead Centurion'. But a Sagbag will make him let down his hair at last, even if he is laughing *at* her rather than *with* her. But he won't like the way she lets down her hair. Under 'Sagittarian Women–Dubious Habits, Volume 234,' it says that Sagbags only shave under their arms if they think the date will lead to a proposal! Well, you can imagine what a Centaur girl in her mid-twenties who's never had a fiancé looks like. She's got waist-length hair that's never touched her head . . .

CAPRICORN MAN – CAPRICORN WOMAN

A tight-fisted miser like Capricorn woman has just got to go for a miracle-worker like J.C. She'll love the way she's only got to buy water for drinks parties, adore the way he can feed thousands with just a few fish . . . But this is also the sign of Humphrey Bogart, and "of all the signs in all the zodiac", this wise guy will only fall for one . . . his own. Every Capricorn knows that anyone who has anything in common with him must be great.

CAPRICORN MAN – AQUARIUS WOMAN

Tricky. The Germaine Greer and Vanessa Redgrave brigade feel quite convinced that God is really a woman. Aquarian men like Barry Humphries are similarly convinced that most men are better off as women, financially anyway. And surely Aquarian Andrew Ridgeley would also count as a big girl. Capricorn men are far more sorted out. Like Al Capone, they'll make sure anyone sharing the same

sign as Valentine's Day will get massacred. So goodbye Aquarius!

CAPRICORN MAN – PISCES WOMAN

Unlikely. Remember Capricorn is the sign of those who walk on water. And a biblical boy is bound to shy away from fish, thinking about Jonah. After all, famous Pisceans in ascending order of size include: Jaws, Orca Killer Whale, Moby Dick and Elizabeth Taylor – all big man-eaters. Early Christians simply adopted the sign of the fish they wore under their collars as a warning, a sort of 'This could happen to you.' The real fisher of men is Pisces woman . . . or was it Pisces hooker?

FUTURE FORECAST

In the coming year, tight-fisted Goats will continue to baffle their dinner guests by roasting just one coffee bean under the grill, while they serve instant!

GEMINI SHOCK

Which Gemini said, 'I'm a bi-sexual . . . if I want sex I have to buy it?' (See Boy George under Gemini).

DO YOU GET ON PEOPLE'S

BORN:

DECEMBER 22nd   Maurice and Robin Gibb, Noel Edmonds, Patricia Hayes.

DECEMBER 23rd   Ava Gardner (something Princess Margaret used to do), Howard Hughes, Helmut Schmidt.

DECEMBER 24th   Kenny Everett, Lou Grade, Noele Gordon, Sissy Spacek, Little Richard, Cynthia Payne.

DECEMBER 25th   Jesus, Humphrey Bogart, Isaac Newton, Annie Lennox.

DECEMBER 26th   Phil Spector, Mao Tse Tung, Thomas Gray.

DECEMBER 27th   Marlene Dietrich, Janet Street-Porter, Gerard Depardieu.

DECEMBER 28th   Maggie Smith, Roy Hattersley, Woodrow Wilson.

DECEMBER 29th   Bernard Cribbins, Magnus Pyke, Marianne Faithfull, Jon Voight, Harvey Smith, Thomas Becket, Radio Luxembourg.

DECEMBER 30th   Tracey Ullman, Rudyard Kipling, Gordon Banks.

DECEMBER 31st   John Denver, Ben Kingsley, Sarah Miles, Andy Summers, Donna Summer.

JANUARY 1st   Idi Amin, J. Edgar Hoover, the first *Top of the Pops*, the Beatles fail their audition with Decca Records, 1962.

JANUARY 2nd   David Bailey, Isaac Asimov.

JANUARY 3rd   Victoria Principal, Victor Borge,

GOAT AS MUCH AS THIS LOT?

	J.R.R. Tolkien, Jane Wyman (*Falcon Crest*), Ronald Reagan's first wife.
JANUARY 4th	Matt Frewer (alias Max Headroom), Dyan Cannon.
JANUARY 5th	Diane Keaton, Robert Duvall, 'Fallon' (*Dynasty*).
JANUARY 6th	Rowan Atkinson, Sacha Distel.
JANUARY 7th	Gerald Durrell.
JANUARY 8th	David Bowie, Elvis Presley, Shirley Bassey, Ron Moody.
JANUARY 9th	Susannah York.
JANUARY 10th	Rod Stewart, Pat Benatar.
JANUARY 11th	Arthur Scargill, Brian Robson.
JANUARY 12th	Michael Aspel, Hermann Goering, Suggs of Madness.
JANUARY 13th	The author of *Paddington*, the author of *Puss in Boots*.
JANUARY 14th	Faye Dunaway, Richard Briers, Albert Schweitzer.
JANUARY 15th	Princess Michael, several Nazis, Frank Bough, Martin Luther King.
JANUARY 16th	Ivan the Terrible, Yuri the Fucking Awful, Sade.
JANUARY 17th	Muhammed Ali, Françoise Hardy, Al Capone, Vidal Sassoon, Benjamin Franklyn, Paul Young.
JANUARY 18th	Cary Grant, David Bellamy, Phil Everley, A. A. Milne.
JANUARY 19th	Janis Joplin, Edgar Allen Poe, Dolly Parton.
JANUARY 20th	George Burns, Malcolm McLaren

Aquarius

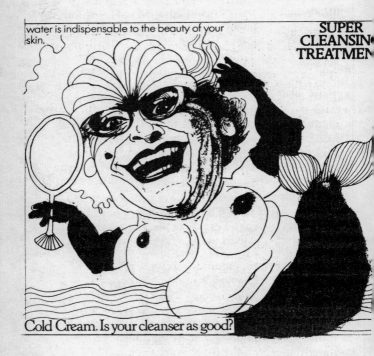

water is indispensable to the beauty of your skin.

SUPER CLEANSING TREATMEN

Cold Cream. Is your cleanser as good?

THE WETTER BORER
JANUARY 1st – FEBRUARY 19th

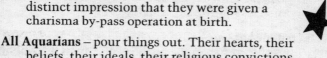

On first impression – all Aquarians leave you with the distinct impression that they were given a charisma by-pass operation at birth.

All Aquarians – pour things out. Their hearts, their beliefs, their ideals, their religious convictions, their political views . . . they are all self appointed 'experts' determined to drown everybody with their monotonous outpourings.

They are – what is commonly known as 'The stuck records of society', The Militant Feminist, the Religious Fanatic, the workman who blames his tools, the mother who tells everybody else how to bring up their children, the DIY know-it-all, the people who always say 'of course I wouldn't have done it like that'.

Their greatest aim – to show that they are right and the rest of the world is wrong. They will bore you to death trying to prove their point.

Famous Wetter Borers include – John 'Isn't-this-game-fun' McEnroe, Germaine 'Tampons-against-the-bomb' Greer, Virginia 'Why-aren't-men-turned-on-by-literary-seminars' Woolf, Vanessa 'I'd-like-to-interrupt-the-Oscars-and-stamp-out-Nazism' Redgrave, and last and least – Ronald 'I-can't-wait-for-my-next-lobotomy' Reagan.

But worst of all – Tony 'Here's another one of my hilarious jokes' Blackburn and Adrian 'Let's-can-Vyvyan's-farts-and-sell-them' Edmonson and Prince 'All-the-gels-love-it-when-I-grin' Andrew.

149

The most sorted out Aquarian – Dame Edna Everage. Still upset at the discovery that her fave flower, the Gladiolus is, like her, an hermaphrodite. Which leads right on to . . .

Famous Aqueerians – Russell 'I-thought-Camp-America-was-San-Francisco' Grant, and Andrew 'When-I-grow-up-I'd-like-to-be-George-Michael's-girlfriend' Ridgley.

Incredible but true – the very first *Desert Island Discs* was broadcast on the birthday of Aquarian Tony Blackburn, the disc jockey everybody would like to see on a desert island.

Unbelievably – the sign of Aquarius, 'The Water-Bearer', is in fact an Air sign, which just goes to show that astrology is a load of bollocks. Except that nobody airs their views quite as much as the Wetter Borer . . .

Fave hobbies include – on holiday, counting the number of grains of sand on the beach, train-spotting, writing down car number plate registrations or, worse still, filing them on the home computer with which every Aquarian can bore you rigid. They also enjoy building the Forth Bridge out of used matchsticks, sticking ten year old holiday photos in albums and methodically labelling each one with a twee caption, like 'Us making the tea' or 'Us putting up the tent', 'Us making another cuppa after putting up the tent'. Aquarian conversation always produces snoring in others.

Typical water-bearer jobs – Fireman (who's come across this sort of case before) Bartender (who will tell you the same joke immediately after he's finished telling it to you for the second time) general Expert and Know-it-all.

AROUND THE HOUSE

Unlike clumsy Sagittarians who don't do anything around the house except walk all over the piles of unwashed underwear, and unlike Leos who haven't heard of 'preparation' before either decorating or sex, Aquarians are the DIY perfectionists whose houses will have fossilised long before they get all those 'little jobs' finished. The direct opposite of Capricorns, who go straight for gloss (in everything) and strictly at odds with Aries, who think undercoats are just for wooftahs.

POLITICS SHOCK
Did you know that Sam Fox shares a birthday with some far bigger tits? (See Jeffrey Archer et al under Aries.)

IN THE CAR

There's nothing an Aquarian likes more than being a car buff, the man who chats endlessly about the fine performance and interior trim of vehicles he will never ever be able to afford. 'Of course, the Ghia 3.2 GT Turbo sixteen valve overhead twin-cam will shift 0–60 in 0.3 and that's a gnat's quicker than the 4.2 six cylinder . . .' These are the people who buy Japanese cars and never stop telling you that they're really just as good as German ones when you take into consideration the ten-speed wipers, the go-fast stripes down the ashtray and the low-profile, two-tone tinny cassette player with auto-rewind, reverse looping and so many other gadgets it never stays still long enough to get through a whole tune . . .

The Drag Coefficient of Aquarian drivers is enormous.

THE PETTY OFFICIALS

If there's one thing an Aquarian loves, it's a rule book with plenty of extra paragraphs and quotable sub-sections. These are the people who design government white papers for fun, the traffic wardens who use phrases like, 'It's more than my job's worth to let you off. Rules is rules.' School prefects, supergrasses, members of the Advertising Standards Authority, the Trades Descriptions people, Driving Examiners – they are all Aquarians. And those are the fun ones. You can always spot an Aquarian when somebody begins a conversation with 'I know it's none of my business, but . . .'

AQUARIUS AND FASHION

These are the people who delight in slogans that try to make a point, the feminist Aquarian will always wear something that says 'Women need men like fish need bicycles'. The Aquarian Real Ale fanatic will always turn up to the pub in a stained, ill-fitting shirt saying, 'My best mate went to a real ale pub and all I got was this Firkin T-shirt.' The Aquarian hippy has countless patched jeans embroidered with the inevitable, 'Today is the first badge of the rest of my life.'

AQUARIUS AND SEX

(Everyone's been bored to sleep listening to their Aquarian partner's theories before anything physical ever crops up.)

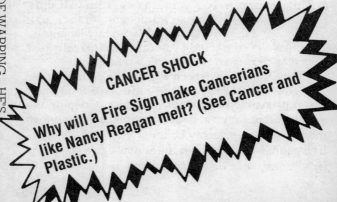

CANCER SHOCK

Why will a Fire Sign make Cancerians like Nancy Reagan melt? (See Cancer and Plastic.)

AQUARIUS MAN

The fate of the world is in the hands of an Aquarius man. This is even more worrying when you consider that this particular individual played alongside a monkey in the film *Bonzo the Chimpanzee*, and the monkey got the better of him. Apart from Ronald Reagan, other Aquarian men include Germaine Greer, Virginia Woolf, Vanessa Redgrave . . . and Dame Edna Everage: all Aquarians at their typically unconventional, outspoken and perverse. Indeed, the subtlest Aquarian man is 'Vyvyan' from *The Young Ones*. Born on January 24th, Adrian 'Vyvyan' Edmonson is Aquarian man at his most polite, merely throwing words like 'bottom-burp' and 'bogey-breath' into the conversation where more typical Aquarians would demonstrate. Nevertheless, Adrian Edmonson displays something of Aquarian Ronnie Reagan's attitude towards foreign policy, particularly his habit of attempting to nuke hippies and wooftahs.

And speaking of Reagan, here's another old joke . . . yes, Aquarians really are the people to whom any astrologer can go up and say, 'Do you realise your movements are ruled by Uranus?' And Ronnie's living proof . . . nobody in the Senate can hear what he's saying when he's sitting down.

AQUARIUS WOMAN

Aquarian Women have a great deal in common with Aquarian men . . . they are both Aquarians and both have hairy chests, five o'clock shadow and athlete's foot, in particular. They are also very unfeminine as a rule, constantly keen to stress that they are at the very least equal to men and, in most cases, superior. Germaine Greer, Vanessa Redgrave and Virginia Woolf are typically strident Aquarian women. Hardly the type to go fluttering their eyelashes in search of a sugar-daddy or approving the stereotyped pin-up and dumb blonde that Aquarian men like Benny Hill and Oliver Reed find intellectually stimulating. Aquarian girls despise the image of Man conveyed by Aquarians like white-suited John Travolta, spoilt little boy John McEnroe, moustachioed bullyboy Burt Reynolds, 'Don't give a damn' Clark Gable, drooling 'Who loves ya, baby?' Telly Savalas or 'Wait till she gets my stick of dynamite down her knickers' Adrian Edmonson. The problem with Aquarian woman is that *she* wants to wear the trousers. *She* wants to be the boss. Just like her male counterpart, she goes into a mega sulk if she can't have things exactly her way. What you're dealing with here is a female McEnroe. With all the broad-mindedness and flexibility of Ronald Reagan. Dame Edna is about as feminine as Aquarian woman gets, and most are nothing like as polite. As for the radical Aquarienne, forget any ideas about her sending you a strip-o-gram in suspenders; Aquarian women only do Greenham-grams: the birthday greeting where a tramp delivers a feminist ultimatum written on a second-hand tampon. (There has never been an Aquarian Miss World or Playmate of the Month.)

TELL-TALE SIGNS

1: Would your Aquarian man be upset if he found you in bed?

2: Does your Aquarian woman know what a bed is?

3: Does your Aquarian woman think a prick is a) an Aquarian man? b) Aquarian Tony Blackburn? c) the male equivalent of brain?

4: Does your Aquarian woman attend seminars in Eunuch-creation?

5: Does your Aquarian man still drop things on floors so he can look up girls' dresses?

6: Is he attracted to lame dogs? (Move on to question seven if you find bestiality repulsive.)

7: Do you share your Aquarian woman's interest in *The Women's Room* and DIY castration?

POP SHOCK

Which Rolling Stone shares a birthday with the Marquis de Sade? (See June 2nd under Gemini.)

Now Available on Traditional Himalayan stereo cassettes . . .
* Beauty from within . . . a complete course in Astral projection and Alopecia. Guaranteed results (some of them good).

✯ AQUARIUS MAN – ARIES WOMAN

Even an Aquarian like Randy Andy will fail to impress an Aries woman. The problem being that they've learned far too much from the men of their own sign . . . It was on March the 31st, under Aries, that the Eiffel tower was fully erected, and French Arietians like Casanova simply said it was a scaled down version of their own towers. Still, Randy Andy can prove himself to be an outstanding prick in practically every other field. Take what he misguidedly calls photography: didn't a critic once say he'd get far better results if he left the lens-cap on . . . ?

☆ AQUARIUS MAN – TAURUS WOMAN

Someone who likes to drown his sorrows as much as Aquarius (remember the sign of the spilling glass) will hardly appreciate a girl born under the same sign as Alcoholics Anonymous, founded on May 12th. Aquarian men like Oliver Reed can't handle Taurean women in love like Glenda Jackson. He's far too fond of having his women underneath. And if she doesn't like it, like fellow-Aquarian Clark Gable, he won't give a damn. The only Aquaman who loves being engulfed in Bull is Ronald Reagan, the ultimate cowboy. So good for Taurus.

AQUARIUS MAN – GEMINI WOMAN

Even a restless Gemini will find an Aquarian man like Bamber Gascoigne too eager to move on. Imagine her disappointment as every night of passion gets reduced to a quickie with his insisting 'I'll have to hurry you on this one . . .' They're all the same. Aquarian Andrew Ridgeley is all 'Wham! Bam! Thank you, ma'am!' He can't bear to lose precious time that

156

could be spent practising soppy looks in the mirror or grovelling to his wet Crab friend, George Michael.

AQUARIUS MAN – CANCER WOMAN

It seems strange that Disneyland opened during Cancer. Cancer is the last place anyone sane would go for amusement. Most Cancerians are far too stay-at-home for adventurous Aquarians, and they won't take kindly to an Aqua-man like Jules Verne of *Twenty Thousand Leagues Under the Sea* trying to explore their hidden depths. Old crabby features is far too possessive. On the other hand, Aquarians like Ronald Reagan just don't have hidden depths; they have hidden shallows . . .

AQUARIUS MAN – LEO WOMAN

What's a lusty Leo lady going to think of a man with the same sign as Kojak? Aquarian men are nearly all as dynamic as lollipop men. Not nearly enough to intrigue a demanding Leo. Even fellow-Leo Alan Whicker hasn't been around as much as many Leo girls. But Aquarian men can be like Boris Spassky, taking eons to make a decision, far too boring for the Leos who love to act first, then think about the consequences later. The only thing Leos have in common with chess players is a love of hard pawn.

AQUARIUS MAN – VIRGO WOMAN

Is a lover of good clean fun going to understand why an Aquarian wally like John Travolta enjoys tossing off his jacket in a disco? And if Aquarian man does hit upon the type of Virgo who really is dirty, she's never going to put up with the outpourings of a man like Bamber Gascoigne constantly quizzing her in bed, 'Where were you last night?' 'What does this one do?' 'Have you been conferring . . . ?'

AQUARIUS MAN – LIBRA WOMAN

Aquarians are certainly unpredictable, but fair-minded Librans will put up with any whim, provided it's under the name of idealism. For instance, if a typical Aqua-man like Ronnie Reagan wants to bomb a load of Libyans in the name of progress, a Libra lady like Maggie will lend him her airports without further consultation. Libras love a bit of argie-bargie. Remember, Mrs T's corner shop was a 'Greengrocers & Warmongers'.

Alternatively, the more peaceful Aquarian/Libra couples, like Andy and Fergie will simply spend year after year trying to show the public more teeth than their partner.

AQUARIUS MAN – SCORPIO WOMAN

With an Aqua-man like Reagan, cunning Scorpio will always take advantage. Just look at the way Scorpio Madame Tussaud sold him her Chamber of Horrors reject, 'Nancy'. Yes, Scorpios are very good at outwitting dummies. They're pretty good at outwitting the few Aquarians with brains as well as brawn. Witness Alan Alda being beaten by Scorpio Loretta 'Hotlips' Swit . . . Alan: 'Nurse, I'd like you to examine between my toes . . . my big toes!' Hotlips soon showed him that Scorpio women do 'come intense', but not the way Aquarian men prefer to spell it . . .

AQUARIUS MAN – SAGITTARIUS WOMAN

Dirty, basic, crude, rude: that's Aquarian man. But he still finds he finds Sagittarian women shocking. You see, Sagbags are never passive in bed. Repulsive maybe, smelly and frequently sick, yes, but never passive. Nobody can keep up with a galloping horse.

AQUARIUS MAN – CAPRICORN WOMAN

Capricious Capricorns are in for a big let-down with Aquarius man. Be warned. The phrase 'Jesus wept' stems from the first time a Capricorn came in contact with an Aquarian joke-teller (an early relative of Aquarian Tony 'I'm-dead-from-the-neck-up' Blackburn).

While Aquarians get a laugh by watching their fellow star Benny Hill, more discerning Capricorns still wonder what the difference is between all his shows. As a rule Aqua-man's sense of humour is rarely understood by others. Take Ronnie Reagan and his 'Princess David' joke . . . nobody in the royal party laughed at all.

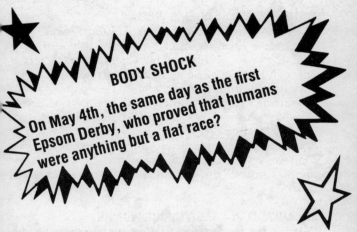

BODY SHOCK

On May 4th, the same day as the first Epsom Derby, who proved that humans were anything but a flat race?

AQUARIUS MAN – AQUARIUS WOMAN

This really is the pits. The John McEnroe/Martina Navratilova match. More than a match for a bad sport like Aquarius, the type that is always convinced of their own right, convinced that the whole of the rest of the world is against them.

No, nobody gets any peace in this relationship, just as they don't with good old Ronnie . . .

AQUARIUS MAN – PISCES WOMAN

An unlikely pairing, just like James Dean and Piscean Liz Taylor in the film *Giant*. He, the slick oil man; she, the typical Piscean dreamer with little grasp of the real world. But Pisces girls always like men in high positions. An Aquarian like Prince 'I've-got-more-teeth-than-most-horses' Andrew can certainly offer those.

But even fish-netted Pisces girls will find Aquarians like Oliver Reed too rude. Like Benny Hill, he aspires to being basic. And Aquarian bastards like Ade Edmonson think the phrase, 'Look, she's a Piscean!', is something you only say to blokes called Ian . . .

IN THE COMING YEAR . . .

Most Aquarians will accept that they do not have inferiority complexes; they simply are inferior.

OCCULT AIDS

is not a disease, but a way of finding harmony and inner life. SEND TODAY for your very own personalised Occult Aid, guaranteed to have the Made in Taiwan sticker removed by craftsmen.

Please state preference:
1. Rare Amik Himalayan stone bangle which turns all nine planets in your favour and will get discount in numerous Indian takeaways.

2. For a further £5 you can have a Himalayan-ish Traditional Sweatshirt embroidered with the ancient saying . . . 'My Mum and Dad saw the light and all I got was this lousy T-shirt.'

ARE YOU AS MUCH OF A

BORN:

JANUARY 21st   Benny Hill, Telly Savalas, Billy
Ocean.

JANUARY 22nd   George Foreman.

JANUARY 23rd   Princess Caroline.

JANUARY 24th   Adrian Edmonson, Natasha Kinski,
Bamber Gascoigne, Neil Diamond,
Jools Holland.

JANUARY 25th   Virginia Woolf, Robbie Burns,
Somerset Maugham.

JANUARY 26th   Eartha Kitt.

JANUARY 27th   Wolfgang Amadeus Mozart, Jerome
Kern.

JANUARY 28th   Alan Alda, Ronnie Scott.

JANUARY 29th   Tony Blackburn, Germaine Greer.

JANUARY 30th   Vanessa Redgrave, John Profumo,
Boris Spassky.

JANUARY 31st   Phil Collins, Norman Mailer.

FEBRUARY 1st   Clark Gable, Terry Jones.

FEBRUARY 2nd   Farah Fawcett, Les Dawson, Nell
Gwynne, Sid Vicious died.

FEBRUARY 3rd   Val Doonican, Doris 'Annie Walker'
Speed.

WETTER BORER AS THIS LOT?

FEBRUARY 4th	Charles Lindbergh.
FEBRUARY 5th	Susan Hill, Robert Peel.
FEBRUARY 6th	Bob Marley, Zsa Zsa Gabor, Ronald Reagan.
FEBRUARY 7th	Charles Dickens, Thomas More.
FEBRUARY 8th	James Dean, Jules Verne.
FEBRUARY 9th	Mia Farrow, Carole King, Holly Johnson.
FEBRUARY 10th	Roberta Flack, Boris Pasternak.
FEBRUARY 11th	Burt Reynolds, Thomas Edison.
FEBRUARY 12th	Charles Darwin.
FEBRUARY 13th	Oliver Reed, Peter Gabriel.
FEBRUARY 14th	'Moneypenny' Lois Maxwell.
FEBRUARY 15th	Galilei Galileo.
FEBRUARY 16th	John McEnroe, *Please Please Me* became The Beatles' first Number One.
FEBRUARY 17th	Dame Edna Everage, Alan Bates, Gene Pitney.
FEBRUARY 18th	John Travolta, Matt Dillon, Len Deighton, Yoko Ono, CND.
FEBRUARY 19th	Prince Randy, Lee Marvin.

Pisces

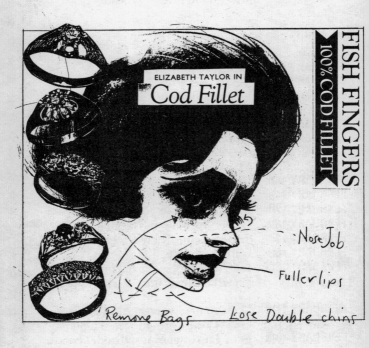

ELIZABETH TAYLOR IN
Cod Fillet

FISH FINGERS
100% COD FILLET

Nose Job

Fuller lips

Lose Double chins

Remove Bags

THE WET DREAMERS
FEBRUARY 20th – MARCH 20th

Famous fish – it cannot simply be a coincidence that their names always lead us back to water . . . Sandie Shaw, Denis Waterman, Mike Love (of the Beach Boys), Handel (of 'The Water Music'), Ros(sea)ni, and Teddy Kennedy, who always mistook driving for diving.

Greatest Pisces fear – hookers.

Fave poets – Shelley, Water de la Mare.

Fave country – Finland.

Pisces and sex – everyone finds 'fish fingers' crumby in bed. But these dreamers *do* get hooked on fantasy . . . don't be surprised if they're captivated by fish-nets and soft prawn. It's generally a very slippery affair.

Typical fish occupations – brain sturgeon, rock star, swimmer, the actors who fail to get parts in *Crossroads*, the people who test suppositories.

On first impression – most Pisces look like normal people seen through fish-eye lenses.

Their lucky day – February 30th.

Fave hobbies – terrapin bowling, skat(e)ing.

Fave hats – straw bloaters.

Pisceans include – most ageing hippies, Ken Dodd's 'diddy men', most garden gnomes, 'Dylan' from *The Magic Roundabout*.

Fave children's names – Bilbo, (or if it's ugly) Gollum, Moonchild, Cat, Jimi . . .

PISCES AND SEX (extended)

Pisces Philip Roth wrote a book called *Portnoy's Complaint*. It could well have been titled 'Pisces Complaint', because the hero, like all Piscean men, turned out to be what is politely referred to as an 'autosexual'. This does not mean that sex comes automatically to a Piscean; simply that his most regular partner is himself. Pisces women are even fishier . . . in fish sex the female fish gives the male a small deposit, then swims off and expects him to squirt all over it! You can get arrested for this sort of behaviour.

Star fish – George Harrison, Rik Mayall, Elizabeth Taylor, Michael Caine.

Rock – Sharkin' Stevens, Peter Fonda, Neil Sedaka, Fats D'minoe, Andy Gibb, Ry Codder . . . all genuine Pisceans.

Sole – Nina Simone, Wilson Pickett.

Kippers – DJ Mike Read who's been to known to do what all sensible people do, i.e. sleep through his own show.

Wet fish – Undoubtedly the wettish fish around is His Royal Wimpiness Prince Edward, the only royal who is so unbelievably uninteresting that he had to send people money to come to his wedding, and even then had to call the whole thing off when the congregation failed to reach the plural. Even his fiancée refused to make it. This entire event was never mentioned in any of the papers because far more interesting stories like the price of butter rising by ½p took its place.

Fave Pisces proverb – Findus Kippers, Losers Weepers.

LET'S GET FISHICAL . . .

The typical Fish is the wet person that always gets battered by everybody else . . . the weed that gets sand kicked in his face on the beach by Aries hearties, the wimp who never stands up to being queue-barged by Sagittarian oafs, the type who can't bear to complain when a Scorpio car mechanic insists that 'Whilst we were doing the oil change, John, we noticed the engine needed changing – and the gearbox – and thought it best to save you money in the future by changing the bodywork and giving it a respray now. That'll be six grand, chief!' The reason for all this is quite simple. It all stems back to Pisceans being ageing hippies, determined to live at peace with the world. After years of turning the other cheek, 'Peace-eans' have developed eyes like fish . . . and the only reason they feel the need to see all around is because they know that in any situation whatsoever, they will be attacked . . . with good cause . . .

THE ANXIETY QUEUER

Picture the scene . . . Pisces man is queueing to see his favourite weepie, *Lassie Come Home* in a double bill with *Woodstock*. The man on the door won't let anyone in until exactly the correct time of opening (he is obviously the petty official breed of Virgo). Pisces man is standing no more than ten back from the front of the queue, but already anxiety is getting the better of him. 'What if the raucous Aries behind barges in front? What if a load of Leos turn up at the last minute and snobbily ignore the whole queueing set-up?' Pisces man is getting in a real panic. Nervously, he inches forward as the person in front leans over. He says nothing as they resume their former position, now standing on his foot. Exactly the same thing happens queueing for the cross channel ferry. Pisces man is convinced that the other lane is edging forward faster than his own. He is terrified that his Mini with the CND and 'NUCLEAR ENERGY? NO THANKS!' stickers will overheat and embarrass him.

Even when he finally gets inside the ferry or the cinema, the anxiety is still there. Pisces people live in permanent fear of loud-mouthed Sagittarians coming up and saying 'Oy! You're sitting in my seat!'

POP SHOCK
Who sensibly left Earth the day David Cassidy appeared? (See Aries, April 7th.)

ROYAL SHOCK
Is Prince Charles really controlled by Martians? (See under Scorpio.)

THE AGEING HIPPY

Unless they can casually slip into inconspicuous light dung-coloured windcheaters and shelter under clubs such as the National Trust, Friends of the Gay Lentil or Trainspotters Anonymous, most Pisceans will harp back to their halycon days in the Sixties, when Country Joe and the Fish got it on, when Yuppies were as unpopular as Guppies, when Sloane Rangers hadn't made it up to town from Gloucestershire because the Range Rover hadn't been invented. These were the days when the free spirit known as Pisces could catch a ride down to Shepton Mallett Festival to see Donovan and convince himself that he was Jack Kerouac on the road. Even today, Pisces man will still have a pair of patched jeans with flared insets in his bottom drawer, to commemorate these good old days. At Christmas parties, the pratts who still turn down the volume so everyone can sing along to the chorus of 'Hi Ho Silver Lining' are Pisceans.

THE INDISPUTABLE PROOF

Nigel Planer, who plays the hippy 'Neil' in *The Young Ones* is a genuine Pisces.

PISCES–SPEAK

Human	Pisces
'Shall we leave now?'	'Let's split.'
'Guitar.'	'Axe.'
'I'd like to tell you about . . .'	'Let me lay this one on you . . .'
'I understand.'	'I've got it sussed, man . . .'

Not surprisingly, all Pisces hippies used to smoke 'Roaches'.

The most dynamic Pisces hero – Leonard Cohen.

ELIZABETH TAYLOR IN
Cod Fillet

FISH FINGERS
100% COD FILLET

Nose Job

Fuller lips

Remove Bags

Lose Double chins

PISCES MAN

The codpiece kid. Yes, if Pisces man ever plucks up enough courage to tell you he's got a whopper, it's just a load of old cod, literally. Though the twelfth sign of the zodiac theoretically comes after all the others, it's just not true . . . Pisces men nearly all suffer from acute premature ejaculation. In conversation it happens when you say 'Mama Cass' or 'Alice B. Toklas'. On dates, it occurs when the girlfriend says, 'Would you like to come back for decaffeinated coffee?' So, if a Pisces ever asks you for coffee, stand well back. These little squirts can often surprise you. And squirts they are . . . there's only one Pisces who's made it to Millionaire's Roe by being tough, Rupert Murdoch, and that fish is a shark . . .

Pisces man has never been the same since the Sixties . . . look at Roger Daltry, the Earl of Snowdon, Neil Sedaka, Rudolf Nureyev . . . speaking of which, these sentimental arty-farty types include some pretty queer fish . . . Frankie Howerd, Kenneth Williams. If Pisces man isn't a drip, he's like Michael Caine and Paul Newman, wishing the Sixties could happen all over again before he reaches his own.

170

PISCES WOMAN

The bird's eye view of fish is much the same. Drips or
60s girls. Jilly Cooper, Jennifer Jones, Samantha Eggar,
Joanne Woodward, Cyd Charisse, Lesley-Ann Down –
nobody under thirty will have heard of them, and
since Flower Power went out of fashion, showbiz has
totally ignored all Pisceans.

Of course today's Pisces woman has swapped
headbands for home-perms that make her look like a
poodle and kaftans have been replaced by Laura
Ashley tents thinly disguised as dresses. But, like
most fish, she's really out of the swim in the
practical, go-getting 80s. There just aren't that many
career opportunities for poets and dream-
interpretation therapists. One or two survive to create
'Haystack' sandwiches for healthfood co-operatives.
All over deepest Devon and Cornwall, Pottery and
Wickerwork Collectives are being run by Piscean
teachers, or as they prefer to be called, 'Wisdom
Sharers'. But generally the vibes are pretty heavy
nowadays and so most Pisces are indulging in their
favourite pastime – drowning their sorrows. Mind
you all Pisces believe in reincarnation, though if that
ever happens, most of them will come back as worry-
beads.

PISCES MAN – ARIES WOMAN

A hot-blooded Aries beauty like Sam Fox or Ali MacGraw is hardly going to be impressed with the eternal Cub-scout Piscean man hoping to turn her on by showing her his knitting proficiency badge and boasting about the size of his 'Woggle'. Any fire sign will find this watery dreamer just too much of a drip. In fact, many claim that the typical Piscean characteristic of being dreamy is just a misspelling . . . the 'M' in dreamy could easily be an 'R'.

PISCES MAN – TAURUS WOMAN

Well, the back to nature Piscean hippy might well become a Friend of the Earth sign Taurus if she's the Earth Mother vegetarian, but most Taurean women prefer red meat to fish. The fact that Piscean man's idea of being outrageous is taking the biggest piece of flapjack on the plate rather than the one nearest to him is hardly going to turn a Taurean like Grace Jones on. For a woman who likes Real Men, fish are hardly a great catch (see Piscean men who like to wear tights in public; under 'Nureyev and other Queer Fish').

PISCES MAN – GEMINI WOMAN

Is a Marilyn Monroe or Joan Collins kind of woman really going to be impressed with a man who turns up to a disco in his trainspotter's anorak and requests anything they've got by Roger Whittaker. Unless you're the type of Fish who doesn't mind girlfriends taking the Pisces out of you, avoid teasing Geminis like the plague. Gemini is the sign of Joan Collins – and Fish always get caught out by hookers.

STAR SHOCK
If you were born between June 22nd and July 23rd, you should avoid jumping in front of trains.

PISCES MAN – CANCER WOMAN

Well, it's hardly very adventurous, going for the first sign that comes along . . . though every Fish must have something in common with a Crab like Prunella Scales. But anyone with a tough shell, like crustacean Diana Rigg, will never take more than a sideways glance at Pisces, the type of man whose favourite martial art is Morris-dancing. Forget it, wimpo! The only Cancer that would give a Pisces a second look was Helen Keller.

PISCES MAN – LEO WOMAN

Leo women throw back the tiddlers; they want a whale of a time – and a big, mean killer whale at that, not the typical Piscean wimp who can turn into a blubber over a poetry reading. Girls like Princess Margaret want caviar . . . the Jackie Onassis type of Leo will only put herself out to very big fish in very big ponds. So, unless you can come up on the pools, forget about Leos. They like to live life to the full, forty-eight hours a day, not daydream like fish. Anyway, they love men who wear furs, not duffel coats, college scarves and Jesus sandals over their socks.

PISCES MAN – VIRGO WOMAN

With the exception of Shirley Conran whose *Lace* heroine got her kicks by shoving goldfish down her pants, Virgo women are just too scheming and practical for the drips who seem totally out of their depth in anything other than abstract dreams. Perhaps you'd see something of yourself in a Virgo like Mary Shelley, but only a similar love of bizarre fantasies. Overall, a critical Virgo girl would find it far too easy to get Pisces baited.

DANCE SHOCK
What do Aquarians toss off in discos?
(See under Travolta.)

PISCES MAN – LIBRA WOMAN

Well, Pisces has certainly got something in common with Libran Maggie Thatcher . . . the old trout . . . and certainly many Librans find it just as hard to make decisions. But the only thing Libran ladies really go fishing for is compliments, to reassure them that people do genuinely like them; something they all get unbalanced about. Sexually? Well, Libran Sylvia Kristel certainly got 'Emmanuelle' to say 'fillet' in the sea a few times, but wouldn't you be worried about catching Herring Aids?

PISCES MAN – SCORPIO WOMAN

You won't find a more different kettle of fish. You may well be soppy and romantic, but a lusty Scorpion will get straight to the point with her sharp tongue. Unlike the typical Pisces who always asks if it will be all right to kiss on the first date (and then it's always written down as part of a poem) a Scorpio girl will just say, 'Whip out your stick,' and shudder as Pisces man produces the walking stick covered in souvenir badges of lakes he has wandered past in Cumbria.

PISCES MAN – SAGITTARIUS WOMAN

Timid little Pisces men do not kiss on the first date. Nor do Sagittarian women – they rape and pillage. These randy animals will laugh till they're hoarse . . . as far as Pisces men, the tiddlers of the zodiac, are concerned, Sagittarian girls are only interested in 'shoal-bangs'. The only type of fish they could possibly accept is one with an Octopus complex, making her feel he had at least eight arms in bed, like a Gemini . . . and even Octopus types will be taken for a load of suckers by insatiable Saggitarius.

PISCES MAN – CAPRICORN WOMAN

This tight-fisted bargain-hunter could be the woman you're looking for . . . most Capricorn women are cheap-skates. But they're also great hypochondriacs and will therefore hate the way Pisces men always say they feel like they've got a cold coming on. Capricorn men are a better bet . . . someone like Magnus Pyke would share a fish's eccentricity. But don't forget Jesus was a Capricorn . . . think how far he stretched those poor little five fishes . . .

PISCES MAN – PISCES WOMAN

Well, a girl like Piscean Jilly Cooper has a mermaid's old-fashioned romantic attitudes. The Liz Taylor variety will certainly join you in drowning your sorrows, but you'd never get beyond the platonic, either because they would spend all night dreaming about it, like you do, or simply because, like the latter example, they'd be too Pisced to do anything about it. No, anyone discovering Pisces man in bed is just going to find a wet blanket . . .

☆ YOUR FUTURE FORECAST

In the coming year, many of you romantic dreamers will turn to Buddhism, because the Buddhists believe in reincarnation and that's got to be better than what you're getting now. The problem is that according to Buddhist legend, one will always return to Earth in the form of something that has been dictated by the way one lives, i.e. if you've lived a better life than most, you will return as something better than most people. If you've lived a bad life, you'll be reincarnated as a lower form of life.

I was talking to a Buddhist skunk the other day . . . he was worried that he'd come back as Maggie Thatcher . . .

ARE YOU AS FISHY

BORN:

FEBRUARY 20th	Sidney Poitier, Enzo Ferrari.
FEBRUARY 21st	Jilly Cooper, Nina Simone, Julie Walters.
FEBRUARY 22nd	Nigel Planer, Bruce Forsyth, Teddy Kennedy, Kenneth Williams, George Washington.
FEBRUARY 23rd	Peter Fonda, Samuel Pepys, Howard Jones.
FEBRUARY 24th	Dennis Waterman, Michel Legrand.
FEBRUARY 25th	John Arlott, George Harrison, Zeppo Marx, Anthony Burgess.
FEBRUARY 26th	Johnny Cash, Fats Domino, Sandie Shaw, Paul Newman.
FEBRUARY 27th	Liz Taylor, Joanne Woodward, John Steinbeck.
FEBRUARY 28th	Barry Fantoni, Blondin.
FEBRUARY 29th	Antonio Rossini, Mario Andretti.
MARCH 1st	Mike Read, Roger Daltrey, Frédéric Chopin, Harry Belafonte, Nik Kershaw.
MARCH 2nd	Jennifer Jones, J. P. R. Williams, Lou Reed.
MARCH 3rd	Jean Harlow, Ronald Searle, Alexander Bell.
MARCH 4th	Patrick Moore, Shakin' Stevens, Antonio Vivaldi.

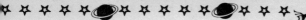

AS THIS LOT?

MARCH 5th	Andy Gibb, Samantha Eggar, Eddy Grant.
MARCH 6th	Michelangelo, Elizabeth Barrett Browning, Frankie Howerd.
MARCH 7th	Rik Mayall, Ivan Lendl, Viv Richards, the Earl of Snowdon.
MARCH 8th	Michael Grade, Cyd Charisse, Kenneth Grahame.
MARCH 9th	Amerigo Vespucci.
MARCH 10th	Prince Edward.
MARCH 11th	Rupert Murdoch, Harold Wilson.
MARCH 12th	Liza Minelli, Nijinsky, Edward Albee.
MARCH 13th	Neil Sedaka, Joe Bugner, Horace Walpole.
MARCH 14th	Michael Caine, Jasper Carrott, Albert Einstein, Quincy Jones.
MARCH 15th	Mike Love.
MARCH 16th	Leo McKern.
MARCH 17th	Lesley-Ann Down, Rudolf Nureyev.
MARCH 18th	Wilson Pickett, Wilfred Owen.
MARCH 19th	Ursula Andress, Philip Roth, Patrick McGoohan.
MARCH 20th	Vera Lynn, Ovid.

AND FINALLY . . . THE PREVIOUSLY UNDISCOVERED 13th SIGN OF THE ZODIAC . . .

Aquariut

THE SIGN OF THE DYSLEXIC
FEBRUARY 29th – FEBRUARY 31st

Fave sexual position – 96 – Soixant-nerd.

Typical occupation – merchant bonker, triffic warden, private defective, landscape hardener, bust conductor, social porker.

Famous Aquariums – Her Majesty the Queer, Discount Linley, Piles Kington, Tony Blackburn.

You can always tell . . . you can always tell an Aquariut by that strange fartaway look in their eyes.

Fave book – *How Greek was my Volley*.

Fave films – *A Horse Called Richard Harris*, Barbaric Streisand's *Mentl*, *Ghostbuggers*.

Fave clothes – For him – A three-piece suite with Gucci toe, ankle boats and executive griefcase. For her – A hump-suit or frying suite with zits up the frent.

Aquariut's drove . . . company cats. After all, these characters tent to get high celeries with plenty of cringe benfits. Typical cars include: Pornche 924 T, Bord Siesta, Dorris Minor.

Aquariut in love – unfartunately, most Aquariuts never fall in love . . . their feeble attempts at reduction are always thwarted by their constantly winking.

Fave pustimes – indoor sperts, horse raping, ten-pin bowelling, a relaxive lunch in a country pube or a Brixton rastarant, inferior decorating, DYI or simply taking the bog for a walk.

Aquariut and politits – mist Aquariuts vote SPD. They love championing the Geace movement. Fave rally – Ban the Comb. Greatest Fear – the nuclear detergent. They are butterly opposed to the armed farces.

Fave TV programmes – *Howard's Gay*, *Eastbenders*, *Shitting Image*, *The Jewel in the Kraut*.

Greatest Aquariut fear – becoming shitzophrenic.

STAR SHOCK

The saddest Aries ever was Arietian Dudley Moore's father. His prayers must have been misheard . . . God gave him a twelve-inch pianist . . .

How to do it

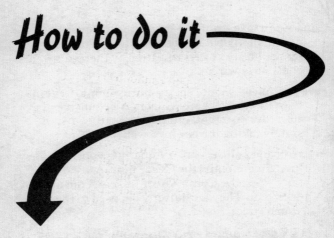

Even without looking up their birthday, there's an absolutely sure-fire way of telling absolutely anybody's true star-sign in an instant. It's easy. Just go up to them and ask them.

YOUR PROBLEMS SOLVED
BEFORE YOU HAVE THEM

Write in complete confidence (of being published) to Astra Agony Aunt . . . CLAIR VOYANT

Dear Clair,
Thank you for replying to my letter before I sent it. However, your answer 'Leave the bugger' did have me rather baffled as my question was actually going to be 'Where's a nice place for a holiday?'

Still, I have acted upon your other forecasts, safe in the knowledge that acting now will avoid future problems ever happening as you predicted. I have therefore divorced my wife to avoid the likelihood of her leaving me at some future date; I told my prospective boss at the interview that I'd had it up to here with working for a tyrant and demanded my gold watch, and I've also had my leg put in plaster anticipating next year's skiing holiday as you so accurately did. But, I'm still not sure about getting into that coffin you sold me . . .

Yours gravely, M. Heseltine, 12 Grosvenor Crescent Mews, W.1.

THE FEMALE STAR-SIGNS

Somebody once said that the Houses of the Zodiac could well be likened to the houses that we choose to live in. Then he fell off his bar-stool. But he had a point; not so much that Capricorns have chimneys or Aries have front doors, but something to do with lifestyle.

- For instance, life with a Sagittarian woman is like a shared house. Hairs in the soap, hairs in the soup, unwashed knickers scattered all over the floor, many with people still wearing them. It's a free-for-all scrum; just the place to find hookers.

- Taurean woman is like a country cottage: warm, cosy, miles away from anything fashionable.

- Gemini woman is like Gemini Joan Collins in bed, a two-up/two-down type of house.

- Aquarian abodes are like Aquarian women. She lives in a flat. Very flat. And constantly on the same level.

- Hygienic Virgo woman is like a spotless house, where you're not even allowed to put ash in the ash-trays.

INTERPRETED AS HOUSES.

- Cancer woman is like a sea-side 'shell'. Full of useless meat.

- Scorpio woman is like a curry restaurant: everyone gets a sting in their tail.

- Pisces woman is like a public swimming-pool: everyone's allowed in, but they all come out wetter than before.

- A Lioness is like a den . . . either full of iniquity or just somewhere for the men to play.

- Libra woman is a semi-detached house. Never fully attached to the people alongside, always keeping a little distance and privacy.

- Aries woman is a terraced cottage, squeezed between men on either side.

- But Capricorn woman is not terraced, semi-detached or even detached. At her most gregarious she lives in a lighthouse. Either setting a shining example or simply ending up on the rocks.

ARE YOU A MONKEY? A CAT? A SKUNK? OR A WOMBAT?

(If so, howcome you are reading a book?)
Find out in this star-studded birthday list . . .

MAGGIE THATCHER	Born in 1483	The year of the Vulture with piles.
PRINCE PHILIP	Born in 1921	The year of the pea-brained Mollusc.
DIANA ROSS	Born in 1944	The year of the Blackbird.
DIRTY DEN	Born in 1947	The year of the Ferret.
IAN BOTHAM	Born in 1955	The year of the Bat.
SIMON LE BON	Born in 1958	The year of the Water-skunk.
JOHN MCENROE	Actually born in 1958, (though he disputes this).	The year of the Vomiting Lark.
PRINCE ANDREW	Born in 1960	The year of the Cheshire Cat.
FRANK BRUNO	Born in 1961	The year of the Urangutang.
ANDREW RIDGELEY	Born in 1963	The year of the Warbling Dickhead.
SAM FOX	Born in 1966	The year of the Greater-spotted Tit.

WHAT THE CHINESE REALLY SAY ABOUT HOROSCOPES . . . .

甲子 日冲 戊午 壬午

甲子 日建 金匱	戊辰 天牢	壬申 青龍 路空
乙丑 天乙 日合	己巳 元武	癸酉 天官 路空
丙寅 喜神 白虎	庚午 司命 日破	甲戌 天刑 旬空
丁卯 玉堂 日刑	辛未 天乙 日害	乙亥 旬空 朱雀

丙寅 日冲 庚申 壬申

戊子 天官 福星	壬辰 金匱 路空	丙申 喜神 日破
己丑 明堂	癸巳 喜神 路空	丁酉 天乙 元武
庚寅 日建 天刑	甲午 白虎	戊戌 福星 旬空
辛卯 朱雀	乙未 玉堂	己亥 天乙 旬空

戊辰 日冲 壬戌 丙戌

壬子 路空 天牢	丙辰 日建 日刑	庚申 福星 金光
癸丑 天乙 路空	丁巳 日祿 明堂	辛酉 日合 寶光
甲寅 司命 不遇	戊午 天刑	壬戌 路空 日破
乙卯 天官 日害	己未 天乙 朱雀	癸亥 玉堂 路空

庚午 日冲 甲子 丙子

丙子 金匱 日破	庚辰 天牢	甲申 日祿 青龍
丁丑 天乙 日害	辛巳 元武	乙酉 明堂
戊寅 日馬 白虎	壬午 天官 路空	丙戌 喜神 旬空
己卯 玉堂	癸未 日合 路空	丁亥 旬空 朱雀

壬申 日冲 丙寅 庚寅

庚子 青龍	甲辰 福星 金匱	戊申 日建 不遇
辛丑 天官 明堂	乙巳 天乙 日合	己酉 元武
壬寅 日馬 日破	丙午 喜神 白虎	庚戌 司命 旬空
癸卯 天乙 路空	丁未 天官 玉堂	辛亥 日馬 旬空

乙丑 日冲 己未 癸未

丙子 天乙 天刑	庚辰 白虎	甲申 天乙 天官
丁丑 日建 朱雀	辛巳 玉堂 不遇	乙酉 勾陳
戊寅 金匱	壬午 天牢 日害	丙戌 喜神 旬空
己卯 日祿 寶光	癸未 路空 日破	丁亥 福星 旬空

丁卯 日冲 辛酉 癸酉

庚子 司命	甲辰 天刑 日害	戊申 白虎
辛丑 勾陳	乙巳 日馬 朱雀	己酉 天乙 日破
壬寅 青龍 路空	丙午 喜神 日祿	庚戌 日合 旬空
癸卯 日建 路空	丁未 寶光	辛亥 天乙 旬空

己巳 日冲 癸亥 丁亥

甲子 天乙 白虎	戊辰 司命	壬申 日合 路空
乙丑 玉堂 不遇	己巳 日建 勾陳	癸酉 路空 朱雀
丙寅 天官 天牢	庚午 日祿 青龍	甲戌 金匱 旬空
丁卯 元武	辛未 福星 明堂	乙亥 日馬 日破

辛未 日冲 乙丑 丁丑

戊子 日害 天刑	壬辰 路空 白虎	丙申 喜神 司命
己丑 日破 朱雀	癸巳 天官 路空	丁酉 日祿 不遇
庚寅 天乙 金匱	甲午 日合 天牢	戊戌 青龍 旬空
辛卯 寶光	乙未 日建 元武	己亥 明堂 旬空

癸酉 日冲 丁卯 辛卯

壬子 日祿 路空	丙辰 日合 天刑	庚申 白虎
癸丑 路空 勾陳	丁巳 天乙 朱雀	辛酉 日建 日刑
甲寅 青龍	戊午 金匱	壬戌 天官 旬空
乙卯 福星 日破	己未 寶光 不遇	癸亥 日馬 旬空

SHEATH-BURSTING ROMANCE!!!

BRUTE!

MALCOLM BENNETT & AIDAN HUGHES

BRUTE!
Colossal, work-hardened men! Wild untameable women!
Savage, unbridled passion! Raw and erotic tales of
gut-wrenching drama and suspense!!

BRUTE!
Romance, cruelty and religion! Sport, crime and agriculture
Horror, western and football!!

BRUTE!
The cult comic of the 80s now unleashed in paperback!

'Unmatched in contemporary British comic art'
CITY LIMITS

'Tough and dirty' THE FACE

'Graphic, gruesome and hilarious' BLITZ

'In future all novels will be written like this' TIME OUT

0 7221 1565 2   CULT/GENERAL FICTION   £1.95

The *true* story of the Cannon Film Empire

HOLLYWOOD A GO-GO

ANDREW YULE

Hollywood film moguls Yoram Globus and Menahem Golan of the Cannon Film Group are a phenomenon of 80s enterprise. With next to no capital and by wheeling and dealing their way up the film industry hierarchy, they have established the Cannon Group as a massive, international film empire.

But the downside of this glittering success story is only now being told. The list of films produced by Cannon includes some of the shoddiest fare ever foisted on the public and most have been box-office disasters. Their accounting methods are under investigation and their sources of finance uncertain. How then have they inspired such confidence in the business world?

In this fascinating and hard-hitting account, Andrew Yule blows the lid off the Cannon go-go boys and provides a unique insight into the more buccaneering aspects of modern entrepreneurial practice.

0 7221 9389 0   NON-FICTION   £3.50

A selection of bestsellers from Sphere

FICTION

THE PRINCESS OF POOR STREET	Emma Blair	£2.99 ☐
WANDERLUST	Danielle Steel	£3.50 ☐
LADY OF HAY	Barbara Erskine	£3.95 ☐
BIRTHRIGHT	Joseph Amiel	£3.50 ☐
THE SECRETS OF HARRY BRIGHT	Joseph Wambaugh	£2.95 ☐

FILM AND TV TIE-IN

BLACK FOREST CLINIC	Peter Heim	£2.99 ☐
INTIMATE CONTACT	Jacqueline Osborne	£2.50 ☐
BEST OF BRITISH	Maurice Sellar	£8.95 ☐
SEX WITH PAULA YATES	Paula Yates	£2.95 ☐
RAW DEAL	Walter Wager	£2.50 ☐

NON-FICTION

NEXT TO A LETTER FROM HOME: THE GLENN MILLER STORY	Geoffrey Butcher	£4.99 ☐
AS TIME GOES BY: THE LIFE OF INGRID BERGMAN	Laurence Leamer	£3.95 ☐
BOTHAM	Don Mosey	£3.50 ☐
SOLDIERS	John Keegan & Richard Holmes	£5.95 ☐
URI GELLER'S FORTUNE SECRETS	Uri Geller	£2.50 ☐

All Sphere books are available at your local bookshop or newsagent, or can be ordered direct from the publisher. Just tick the titles you want and fill in the form below.

Name_____

Address_____

_____

Write to Sphere Books, Cash Sales Department, P.O. Box 11, Falmouth, Cornwall TR10 9EN

Please enclose a cheque or postal order to the value of the cover price plus:

UK: 60p for the first book, 25p for the second book and 15p for each additional book ordered to a maximum charge of £1.90.

OVERSEAS & EIRE: £1.25 for the first book, 75p for the second book and 28p for each subsequent title ordered.

BFPO: 60p for the first book, 25p for the second book plus 15p per copy for the next 7 books, thereafter 9p per book.

Sphere Books reserve the right to show new retail prices on covers which may differ from those previously advertised in the text elsewhere, and to increase postal rates in accordance with the P.O.